Sacred Rhetoric

SACRED RHETORIC

*Preaching as a
Theological and Pastoral Practice
of the Church*

Michael Pasquarello III

WILLIAM B. EERDMANS PUBLISHING COMPANY
GRAND RAPIDS, MICHIGAN / CAMBRIDGE, U.K.

Wm. B. Eerdmans Publishing Co.
255 Jefferson Ave. S.E., Grand Rapids, Michigan 49503 /
P.O. Box 163, Cambridge CB3 9PU U.K.

Printed in the United States of America

10 09 08 07 06 05   7 6 5 4 3 2 1

Library of Congress Cataloging-in-Publication Data

Pasquarello, Michael.
Sacred rhetoric: preaching as a theological and pastoral practice of the church /
Michael Pasquarello III.
p.   cm.
Includes bibliographical references.
ISBN-10 0-8028-2058-1 / ISBN-13 978-0-8028-2058-7 (pbk.: alk. paper)
1. Preaching — History.   I. Title.

BV4207.P29   2005
251'.009 — dc22

2005050715

www.eerdmans.com

Contents

CONTENTS

Preface

This book does not presume to say anything new about the practice of preaching; I have written it in order to show a way to think with the past to live out of it into the future. In so doing, I hope to provide an alternative to the conventional wisdom in our time that says we just need to devise some "new ideas" about "how to" make church talk more culturally relevant, interesting, entertaining, and so on. According to the witness of Scripture, the perennial challenge of Israel and the church is not irrelevance; it is idolatry. Our most "deeply felt need" as God's people is for fidelity to the One who lovingly calls and redeems us through the Word and Spirit to bear faithful witness in the world through a common life of thankful praise and adoration.

I have also written this book to engage in the current discussion concerning the "problem" with preaching and what should be done to fix it. I hope to demonstrate by means of historical examples that the most serious challenges surrounding preaching can be attributed to its separation from the larger story of the church and the full range of Christian practices — doctrine, biblical exegesis, worship, spirituality and the moral life, and so forth. In other words, modernity's redefining of the historical practice or craft of preaching as a distinct discipline within the theological curriculum — homiletics — has succeeded. A consequence, however, is that, for many, preaching has been reduced from a sacrament of divine-human conversation, which end is communion, to a technical procedure for the transmission of religious or moral information, which end is consumption. Yet listeners still long to hear preachers speak of God and the things of God as an expression of godly wisdom.

The idea for this book emerged from a seminar in the history of preaching offered at Duke Divinity School and Asbury Theological Seminary. I am deeply grateful to Sam Eerdmans and the William B. Eerdmans Publishing Company for their enthusiastic support of my proposal. In addition, I am indebted to Dr. Peter Iver Kaufman for supervising my doctoral work in the history of preaching, for his wisdom as teacher and example as scholar. I owe many thanks to Lance Lazar, David Steinmetz, Richard Lischer, John Wall, Stanley Hauerwas, William Willimon, and William Turner for guiding, challenging, and affirming my interests in both the preaching tradition and the field of homiletics. My colleagues at Asbury Theological Seminary, especially in Preaching and Worship, have welcomed and encouraged me with their interest and suggestions. A special word of gratitude goes to my Academic Dean, Joel B. Green, who has such a good "ear" for the grammar of preaching. And I would love to simply say thank you to Mary Hietbrink and Andrew Hoogheem for their excellent editorial assistance in bringing this book to completion.

Finally, I believe it is more than coincidental that I began to think seriously about preaching as a theological and pastoral practice while serving as minister of the Oleander and Devon Park United Methodist Churches in Wilmington, North Carolina, from 1987 to 1991. These two small congregations, struggling to be faithful despite constant temptation to make institutional survival an end in itself, shared with me the best gift a preacher could hope to receive: the expectation that I show up each Sunday prepared to speak of God. I dedicate this book to them with much gratitude.

Preaching in Communion

Sacred Rhetoric: Preaching as a Theological and Pastoral Practice of the Church is an essay in homiletic theology, a description of the enactment of Christian witness, the performance of God's Word through the ministry of preaching. Selected sketches from the Christian tradition display the practice of preaching as shaped by theological wisdom, a form of primary theology that creates and sustains the church by nurturing and testing its faith. Focusing on the work of salutary exemplars within the communion of saints, this book is an invitation to join an extended conversation with the past in order to become more faithful speakers of the Gospel today. It is written with the conviction that our recovery of the homiletic tradition is integral to the restoration of a robust, unreservedly Christian witness for the task of evangelization and ecclesial formation in the post-Christian, missionary situation in which we find ourselves.[1]

Because a single picture has increasingly held captive the homiletic imagination of the church in late modernity[2] — that of technical or sci-

---

1. For assistance in thinking through this project, I am indebted to Stephen E. Fowl and L. Gregory Jones, *Reading in Communion: Scripture and Ethics in Christian Life* (Grand Rapids: Eerdmans, 1991). On the significance of describing the history of Christian practice as a guide for the present, see George A. Lindbeck, "Atonement and the Hermeneutics of Intratextual Social Embodiment," in *Evangelicals and Postliberals in Conversation*, ed. Timothy R. Phillips and Dennis L. Okholm (Downers Grove, Ill.: InterVarsity Press, 1996). See the argument for the recovery of tradition in Jaroslav Pelikan, *The Vindication of Tradition* (New Haven: Yale University Press, 1984).

2. See the excellent summary in James Kay, "Reorientation: Homiletics as Theologically Authorized Rhetoric," *Princeton Seminary Bulletin* 24, no. 1 (2003): 16-35. See also

entific reason rather than theological wisdom — I hope to enlarge our contemporary discussion by introducing select exemplars from Augustine to John Calvin. Rather than devising new techniques or strategies for effective communication, this book invites attention to exemplary figures in the church's company of preachers for whom the ministry of Christian speech was learned through prayerful, studied attention to the Bible, and for whom Scripture in its relationship to the Triune God and the economy of salvation was a "living and active" instrument of divine self-revelation.[3]

In response to our contemporary "forgetfulness of the Word," the all-too-easy, even irreverent, idle chatter that does little serious work in speaking of the God of the Gospel, I hope to suggest an alternative way of seeing the practice of Christian preaching, a recovery of homiletic imagination shaped by scriptural memory, colored by moral judgment, and constituted by participation in a living tradition. Believing that our time is characterized by the extent to which ingenuity has outstripped wisdom, I sketch portraits of virtuous readers and speakers of the Word whose wisdom may guide us in summoning the church to go on in performing its faith in the Triune God.[4]

In *An Essay in the Grammar of Assent*, John Henry Newman wrote of the importance of imitating the character and practical wisdom demonstrated by others:

> Instead of trusting logical science, we must trust persons, namely those who by long acquaintance with their subject have a right to

---

Charles L. Campbell, *Preaching Jesus: New Directions for Homiletics in Hans Frei's Postliberal Theology* (Grand Rapids: Eerdmans, 1997).

3. See the excellent study by Telford Work, *Living and Active: Scripture in the Economy of Salvation* (Grand Rapids: Eerdmans, 2002). See also Kevin J. Vanhoozer, "Scripture and Tradition," in *The Cambridge Companion to Postmodern Theology*, ed. Kevin J. Vanhoozer (Cambridge: Cambridge University Press, 2003), pp. 149-69; John Webster, *Holy Scripture: A Dogmatic Sketch* (Cambridge: Cambridge University Press, 2003), pp. 68-106; David S. Yeago, "The Bible," in *Knowing the Triune God: The Work of the Spirit in the Practices of the Church*, ed. James J. Buckley and David S. Yeago (Grand Rapids: Eerdmans, 2001), pp. 60-66.

4. I am indebted to the larger discussion of these and related matters in Nicholas Lash, *The Beginning and the End of Religion* (Cambridge: Cambridge University Press, 1996). See also the extended discussion in Robert L. Wilken, *Remembering the Christian Past* (Grand Rapids: Eerdmans, 1995); Stephen R. Holmes, *Listening to the Past: The Place of Tradition in Theology* (Grand Rapids: Baker Academic, 2002).

judge. And if we wish ourselves to share in their convictions and the grounds of them, we must follow their history, and learn as they have learned. We must ... depend on practice and experience more than on reasoning. ... By following this we may ... rightly lean upon ourselves, directing ourselves by our own moral and intellectual judgment, not by our skill in argumentation.[5]

Accordingly, preaching as "sacred rhetoric" is a Christian practice that requires the formation of a certain kind of person capable of exercising theological and pastoral wisdom, a form of discernment that includes, but also transcends, the use of technique and skill; for the more that external tasks of ministry are focused upon as the primary goal of theological training and ecclesial vocation, the less pastors will be qualified to carry them out.

This paradox is grounded in the Gospel itself; for if, in our desire to be effective, relevant, or successful, we reduce pastoral ministry to the acquisition of the latest "how to" ideas and strategies, we quickly forget the mystery of divine revelation and the working of grace that are necessary to make sacred rhetoric truly sacred as the Word of God. As a Christian practice, preaching is dependent on the power and wisdom of God to redeem human speech to become an instrument of divine discourse, a graced capacity for "knowing how" to speak the language and grammar of faith embodied in the church's Scripture, story, worship, and common life.[6]

---

5. Newman, cited in Joseph Dunne, *Back to the Rough Ground: Practical Judgment and the Lure of Technique* (Notre Dame: University of Notre Dame Press, 1993), p. 35.

6. I am not using the term "sacred rhetoric" in a technical or academic sense; I am using it to call attention to the theological nature of preaching as an activity of personal address by God in human speech; both a gift received and a response evoked by the mystery of Divine Speech: God's Word incarnate in Christ, embodied in Scripture, echoed in sermons, and enacted by the church for the sake of the world. See the classic description of sacred Scripture and sacred doctrine in Henri de Lubac, *Medieval Exegesis: The Four Senses of Scripture*, vol. 1, trans. Mark Sebanc (Grand Rapids: Eerdmans, 1989), pp. 1-116; see also Work, *Living and Active*, p. 59; Vanhoozer, "Scripture and Tradition," pp. 164-66. In addition, see the historical study in Deborah K. Shuger, *Sacred Rhetoric* (Princeton: Princeton University Press, 1988). On theology as the knowledge of God, a gift of divine wisdom that leads to salvation, see Edward Farley, *Theologia: The Fragmentation and Unity of Theological Education* (Philadelphia: Fortress Press, 1983), pp. 127-29; Edward Farley, *Practicing Gospel: Unconventional Thoughts on the Church's Ministry* (Louisville: Westminster/John Knox, 2003), pp. 93-107; Stephen H. Webb, *The Divine Voice: Christian Proclamation and the Theology of Sound* (Grand Rapids: Brazos Press, 2004), pp. 165-98.

Moreover, the church's reading and speaking of the Word found in Scripture is guided by doctrine, the grammar, rule, or stage direction for enactment of the story that calls it into being: the life, death, and resurrection of Jesus Christ. This is a form of practical knowledge, which leads to wisdom; doctrine is simply the rule and discipline of the practice, which grew out of the baptismal creeds and "rules of faith" in the early church. All later developments — the creeds of the ecumenical councils, the *summa* of the medieval period, and sixteenth-century Protestant and Catholic confessions of faith — are no different in intent: to rule the proper and faithful telling and following of Christ's story in the life of the church.

Doctrine is therefore the necessary grammar of Christian discourse that helps to protect correct reference to God and disciplines our propensity to idolatry.[7] Its purpose is to show how the language of faith may best fulfill its own aim, which is to serve as the language of the Holy Spirit, the language in which God addresses us to effect what is spoken. As Nicholas Lash notes, "The performance of scripture *is* the life of the church."[8]

For much of the church's life, preaching has been viewed as a "storied" practice, a homiletic form of pastoral theology enacted within the liturgy of the church, oral testimony articulated from within the ongoing, lively conversation between doctrine and Scripture — not as something standing alongside them as another discipline. "The church's faith and life were seen as continuous with the biblical narrative, and the Scriptures were interpreted within the context of a living theological and spiritual tradition. The Bible was the book of the church, and its interpretation was to be shaped by the church's faith."[9]

From the early church through the sixteenth century, theology — *theologia* — was a practical habit, a *habitus*; it was an aptitude of the soul, the human intellect, and the heart, having the primary characteristic of wisdom. In earlier times, some saw this more as a directly infused gift of God, tied directly to faith, prayer, virtue, and a desire for God. Later, with the advent of formal theological investigation, others saw it as a wisdom

---

7. Gerard Loughlin, "The Basis and Authority of Doctrine," in *The Cambridge Companion to Christian Doctrine*, ed. Colin E. Gunton (Cambridge: Cambridge University Press, 1997), pp. 52-57.

8. Lash, *Theology on the Way to Emmaus* (London: SCM Press, 1986), p. 43.

9. Robert L. Wilken, "In Defense of Allegory," in *Theology and Scriptural Imagination*, ed. L. Gregory Jones and James J. Buckley (Oxford: Blackwell, 1998), p. 48.

that could also be promoted, deepened, and extended by human study and argument. The meaning of theology, however, did not displace the more primary sense of the term: theology as a practical *habitus*, as knowledge whose end is salvation, wisdom that orders our personal and common life toward God and the things of God.[10]

Acquired through prayerful study of Scripture according to the rule of faith, theology is exegetical, and exegesis is theological; the end or goal is moral and spiritual: the holiness of the church through participation in the life of God.[11] When knowledge of God is proclaimed through the language of faith and interpreted according to its grammar through a "means of grace" such as preaching, it too is part of the activity of theology in a primary, ecclesial sense. Within a common life shaped by sermons, hymns, liturgy, devotion, and discipleship, people become Christian by believing and obeying the first-person language of the Bible and making themselves at home in it; when theology is personally appropriated and absorbed, its hearers are disposed to godliness.[12]

The Division of Theology and Preaching

The Enlightenment imagined reason's sovereignty to rule not only its domain but also everything else, which transformed, respectively, the foundation of Christian teaching and preaching — Scripture and tradition — into history and experience, and left a liberal theology (and its correlative homiletic) that is finally no theology at all. Scripture was no longer understood as mutually constituted by the story it narrates and the community to whom it is narrated — a community already contained within the story, as the story within it. Rather, the historical and scientific study of Scripture left it as unreliable, and thus looked elsewhere to validate the historical events behind the text, which could be available to anyone possessing an appropriately informed interest. That Scripture, as the church's canon, should be the subject of theological and pastoral wisdom in its li-

---

10. Farley, *Theologia*, pp. 33-39. See also the survey and definition of theology in Aidan Nichols, O.P., *The Shape of Catholic Theology: An Introduction to Its Sources, Principles, and History* (Collegeville, Minn.: Liturgical Press, 1991).

11. See the excellent discussion in William M. Thompson, *The Struggle for Theology's Soul: Contesting Scripture in Christology* (New York: Crossroad Publishing, 1996), pp. 1-32.

12. Paul L. Holmer, *The Grammar of Faith* (San Francisco: Harper & Row, 1978), pp. 203-4.

turgical enactment and ecclesial embodiment was no longer required, since historical criticism, guided by reason, became the new foundation for establishing the basis of Christian teaching.

Tradition was treated in a similar manner since, due to a growing suspicion of the accumulated wisdom of the Christian past, it was seen as insufficient for the radically homogeneous world of modernity in which knowledge rests upon the consciousness of the moment. Instead of appealing to Scripture and its interpretation according to the conversations of the past, it was deemed superior to make direct appeal to the experience of fundamentally isolated individuals, since it has the value of being of the moment. Lost, however, was the most important factor that actually constitutes the religious experience of most people: the communal traditions of story, belief, and practice, of liturgy and ritual, and in the case of the church, the theological witness of Scripture that shapes and molds the character of Christian people within the medium of a shared language and life.[13]

In addition to transforming Scripture into history and tradition into experience, modernity eventually divided theology as practical knowledge of God into separate disciplines within the university curriculum. *Theologia,* that unifying habit of salvation-disposed wisdom, a gift of divine revelation and studied obedience to Scripture according to its Trinitarian grammar, instead became the practical know-how necessary to ministerial tasks, a technical and specialized scholarly undertaking among others, now known as "systematic" theology. This development, in turn, created the need for a separate discipline called "ethics," which only served to increase further the separation of doctrine from the practices of the church, the knowledge of God from the life of God's people.[14]

13. Here I have followed the excellent discussion in Loughlin, "The Basis and Authority of Doctrine," pp. 43-52; Stephen E. Fowl, "Introduction," in *The Theological Interpretation of Scripture* (Cambridge, Mass.: Blackwell, 1997); Webster, *Holy Scripture,* pp. 117-22.

14. Farley, *Theologia,* pp. 52-67. On the division of doctrine and ethics, see Stanley M. Hauerwas, "On Doctrine and Ethics," in *The Cambridge Companion to Christian Doctrine,* ed. Gunton, pp. 41-64; Stanley M. Hauerwas, "Christians in the Hands of Flaccid Secularists: Theology and 'Moral Inquiry' in the Modern University," in *Sanctify Them in the Truth* (Nashville: Abingdon, 1998). See also David H. Kelsey, *To Understand God Truly: What's Theological about a Theological School* (Louisville: Westminster/John Knox Press, 1992), pp. 78-102; Hans W. Frei, *Types of Christian Theology,* ed. George Hunsinger and William C. Placher (New Haven: Yale University Press, 1992), pp. 92-146.

In the wake of the Enlightenment, the theological school became a plurality of sciences, an aggregate of scholarly pursuits. Theology was no longer a gift of grace, knowledge/wisdom of God that embraces all of life, but one specialty, an assortment of beliefs that creates the problem of discerning practical ends beyond itself and the means of obtaining those ends. Once theology is thought of as being simply a deposit, a collection of truths or beliefs, theory/practice in the modern sense is born; the challenge of building a bridge from those truths to practical situations is created, and the question of contemporary relevance gains prominence over the worship of God and formation of Christian faith, identity, and mission. Viewed no longer as Christian wisdom that shapes the mind and heart of the church, theology is transformed into theory measured by its usefulness, just as Scripture is reduced to text, a source book from the past out of which ideas and morals can be extracted and applied according to criteria extrinsic to Christian convictions required for its ecclesial use.[15]

The professionalization of clerical education also contributed to the institutionalization of the division of the theological disciplines, formally separating theology and biblical study and reorienting them toward the criteria established by their respective academic guilds, thus distancing both from ecclesial practice.[16] A consequence of these developments was that the field of homiletics as a practical discipline within the ministerial curriculum was shaped more by dependence upon the practice of rhetoric than theologically and liturgically informed ways of reading and speaking Scripture.[17] Severed from the mystery of God, the church's

15. Farley, *Theologia*, pp. 72-139. See the discussion of modern biblical scholarship and use of the Bible in the church in Stanley M. Hauerwas, *Unleashing the Scripture: Freeing the Bible from Captivity to America* (Nashville: Abingdon Press, 1993), pp. 15-46; Robert Louis Wilken, "In Defense of Allegory," in *Theology and Scriptural Imagination*, ed. Jones and Buckley, pp. 35-49; Webster, *Holy Scripture*, pp. 107-35; Eugene H. Peterson, *Working the Angles: The Shape of Pastoral Integrity* (Grand Rapids: Eerdmans, 1987), pp. 61-102.

16. Fowl, "Introduction," in *The Theological Interpretation of Scripture*, pp. xii-xvi.

17. See the discussion of the theological disciplines and their integration in Charles M. Wood, *Vision and Discernment: An Orientation in Theological Study* (Atlanta: Scholars Press, 1985), pp. 1-37. On the predominance of rhetorical rather than theological authority in homiletic practice, see Kay, "Reorientation: Homiletics as Theologically Authorized Rhetoric." See also the following essays in the *Concise Encyclopedia of Preaching*, ed. William H. Willimon and Richard Lischer (Louisville: Westminster/John Knox Press, 1995): O. C. Edwards, "History of Preaching," pp. 217-22; Don M. Wardlaw, "Homiletics and Preaching in

story, its doctrinal and exegetical tradition, sermon production was increasingly guided by individualistic, abstract, a-historical aims, thus surrendering the distinctive theological content and purpose by which Christian preaching and Christian life might be distinguished from other forms of speech and corporate life.[18]

Most significantly, this "clerical paradigm" placed an inordinate amount of emphasis on the activity, control, and power of a single expert; a professional person separated from the church's historically mediated theological wisdom could easily become captive to more seemingly pressing and culturally determined concerns. Operating within the "theory and practice" split of modernity, homiletic practice was rendered vulnerable to being co-opted for the pursuit of predetermined ends, reduced to formulaic design, and valued primarily for its utility in effecting desired outcomes extrinsic to the story of the Gospel and church.[19] Preaching that aims to be "culturally relevant" may just be that, culturally relevant; but this is no guarantee that it is Christian preaching. Eugene Peterson observes,

> The secularized mind is terrorized by mysteries. Thus it makes lists, labels people, assigns roles, and solves problems. But a solved life is a reduced life. These tightly buttoned up people never take great faith risks or make convincing love talk. They deny or ignore the mysteries and diminish human existence to what can be managed, controlled, and fixed. We live in a cult of experts who explain and solve. The vast tech-

North America," pp. 242-52; Conrad Harry Massa, "Homiletics: Teaching of, Graduate Study, Professional Associations," pp. 255-57; Richard C. Stern, "Pedagogy of Preaching," pp. 367-68; Craig L. Loscalzo, "Rhetoric," pp. 411-16. See also Richard Lischer's critique of preachers' reliance on rhetoric in place of the power of the Gospel in "Resurrection and Rhetoric," in *Marks of the Body of Christ*, ed. Carl E. Braaten and Robert W. Jenson (Grand Rapids: Eerdmans, 1999), pp. 13-24.

18. See the discussion in Craig Dykstra, "Reconceiving Practice in Theological Inquiry and Education," in *Virtues and Practices in the Christian Tradition*, ed. Nancey Murphy, Brad J. Kallenberg, and Mark Theissen Nation (Harrisburg, Pa.: Trinity Press International, 1997), pp. 161-84.

19. Dykstra, "Reconceiving Practice in Theological Inquiry and Education," pp. 164-66. See the discussion of therapeutic forms of Christianity in L. Gregory Jones, "The Psychological Captivity of the Church in the United States," in *Either/Or: The Gospel or Neopaganism*, ed. Carl E. Braaten and Robert W. Jenson (Grand Rapids: Eerdmans, 1995), pp. 97-112.

nological apparatus around us gives the impression that there is a tool for everything if we only can afford it. Pastors cast in the role of spiritual technologists are hard put to keep that role from absorbing everything else, since there are so many things that need to be and can, in fact, be fixed.[20]

Toward Reconciling the Division

So long as preaching is seen as a technical procedure or skill rather than an ecclesial practice that is intrinsically shaped within a larger world of theological wisdom, it will yield to more pragmatic and utilitarian concerns for "relevant" or "effective" communication that focuses on packaging and presenting religious information. Lacking the particular theological and pastoral substance and scope of Christian convictions, preachers will continue to be tempted to excessively spiritualized or moralized forms of speech that render God without a people and a people without God.[21]

We are in need of an alternative to the "story of modernity." This will not come, however, in the form of new communication theories, evangelistic strategies, sermon styles, or presentational technologies, but rather through the re-traditioning of our homiletic imagination.[22] Thomas Long comments,

> When the preacher goes to the scripture, new ground is not being broken. The church has been to this text before — many times — and a

20. Eugene Peterson, *The Contemplative Pastor: Returning to the Art of Spiritual Direction* (Grand Rapids: Eerdmans, 1989), p. 64.

21. Quentin Schultze refers to this form of communication as "messaging," which is abstracted from intimacy, tradition, community, and wisdom. Quentin J. Schultze, *Habits of the High-Tech Heart: Living Virtuously in the Information Age* (Grand Rapids: Baker Academic, 2002). See the description of culturally accommodated preaching within mainline churches in William H. Willimon, *The Intrusive Word: Preaching to the Unbaptized* (Grand Rapids: Eerdmans, 1994), pp. 15-26. For a good discussion of evangelistic strategies among seeker-sensitive churches, see Todd E. Johnson, "Truth Decay: Rethinking Evangelism in the New Century," in *The Strange New Word of the Gospel: Re-evangelizing in the Postmodern World,* ed. Carl E. Braaten and Robert W. Jenson (Grand Rapids: Eerdmans, 2002), pp. 118-39.

22. On the failure of modern communication theory and technique, see John Durham Peters, *Speaking into the Air: A History of the Idea of Communication* (Chicago: University of Chicago Press, 1999). See the critical discussion of technique and the argument for a return to the "rough ground" of tradition and practice in Dunne, *Back to the Rough Ground.*

theological tradition, is, in part, the church's memory of past encounters with this and other biblical texts. A theologically informed interpreter of scripture enters the text guided by a text from a theological tradition; the interpreter arrives not as a disoriented stranger but as a pilgrim returning to a familiar land, recognizing old landmarks and thereby alert for new and previously unseen wonders.[23]

By listening to our Christian past, we may begin to discern the particular intellectual, moral, and devotional virtues displayed by wise exemplars for whom Christian speech, informed by the "grammar of faith," did the necessary work to glorify God and to edify the church to participate in God's mission to the world.[24] This will require us to enlarge the circle of our contemporary homiletic conversation to include forgotten "others" from the communion of saints, a form of Christian remembering: an awareness of the history of the church as the story of our life. Such remembering, moreover, may assist us in cultivating virtues of constancy and hope to go on speaking of God and the things of God to a church in search of its way during uncertain times.[25]

An Invitation to Join a Conversation

The following chapters are an invitation to join a conversation with selected members of the "company of preachers" who made significant contributions to Christian renewal and reform.[26] The sketches of these

23. Long, *The Witness of Preaching* (Louisville: Westminster/John Knox Press, 1989), p. 53.

24. On the role of masters, the virtues, and imitation in learning a practice or craft, see Alasdair MacIntyre, *Three Rival Versions of Moral Enquiry: Encyclopedia, Genealogy, and Tradition* (Notre Dame: University of Notre Dame Press, 1990), pp. 65-66.

25. Henri de Lubac, *Medieval Exegesis: The Four Senses of Scripture*, vol. 2, trans. E. M. Macierowski (Grand Rapids: Eerdmans, 2000), pp. 217-18. See also the excellent introduction in Ellen Charry, *By the Renewing of Your Minds: The Pastoral Function of Christian Doctrine* (New York: Oxford University Press, 1997), pp. 3-34; John Leith, "The Significance of the History of Doctrine for Theological Study," in *Theology in the Service of the Church: Essays in Honor of Thomas W. Gillespie*, ed. Wallace M. Alston Jr. (Grand Rapids: Eerdmans, 2000), p. 132.

26. I gladly acknowledge the limitations of my selections. However, my purpose is not to be comprehensive; that is, I am not writing an inclusive history of preaching, but rather presenting particular "case studies" from which we might better learn to study the history of our practice. Given the nature of this kind of study, the characters selected could have

individuals do not presume to be comprehensive, but rather to provide brief descriptions of a larger story and world informed by Trinitarian faith and life, the unifying *habitus* of theology, the knowledge and love of God in its various modes of ecclesial expression.

Because they are exemplars of Christian wisdom, a "family practice" style of theology, a living communion binds their work: a coherence between the interpretation of doctrine and Scripture, and between Scripture and church, grounded in and continuous with the living narrative of Christ and his people. This theological and spiritual tradition "nourished their language and grammar, informed their imaginations, and, most important, transformed their lives and speech."[27] There were imperfections, which in some cases could be quite glaring; theological differences, which in certain matters were considerable; and a diversity of historical circumstances and conditions, which at times were substantial. Still, the one, all-embracing providential story of the present and past dealings of the Triune God with God's people and God's world remained their natural habitat for reading, speaking, and obeying Scripture: "The Bible was the book of the church, and the church was a people of the book; its use shaped and was shaped by doctrine, worship, and life."[28]

---

been otherwise. It is my hope that more historians and homileticians will join in this kind of work. For an example of inviting readers into a conversation with the Christian past, see Luke Timothy Johnson and William S. Kurz, S.J., *The Future of Catholic Biblical Scholarship: A Constructive Conversation* (Grand Rapids: Eerdmans, 2002), pp. 3-63. Stephen E. Fowl asserts, "Pre-modern scriptural interpretation should be seen as a conversation partner providing insights and resources for reading scripture theologically in the present" ("Introduction," in *The Theological Interpretation of Scripture*, p. xvii). See also Stanley Grenz and John R. Franke, "Theological Heritage as Hermeneutical Trajectory: Towards a Nonfoundationalist Understanding of the Role of Tradition in Theology," in *Ancient and Postmodern Christianity: Paleo-Orthodoxy in the Twenty-First Century: Essays in Honor of Thomas C. Oden*, ed. Kenneth Tanner and Christopher A. Hall (Downers Grove, Ill.: InterVarsity Press, 2002).

27. Marva Dawn and Eugene Peterson, *The Unnecessary Pastor: Rediscovering the Call* (Grand Rapids: Eerdmans, 2000), p. 65. See also the excellent discussion of pre-modern "family practice" theology in William M. Thompson, *The Struggle for Theology's Soul: Contesting Scripture in Christology* (New York: Crossroad Publishing, 1996), pp. 1-15.

28. Robert L. Wilken, "In Defense of Allegory," in *Theology and Scriptural Imagination*, ed. L. Gregory Jones and James J. Buckley (Oxford: Blackwell, 1998), p. 48. See also Fowl, "Introduction," in *The Theological Interpretation of Scripture*, pp. xvi-xix; George Lindbeck, "Scripture, Consensus, and Community," in *The Church in a Postliberal Age*, ed. James J. Buckley (Grand Rapids: Eerdmans, 2002), pp. 212-17; Ephraim Radner, *Hope among the Fragments: The Broken Church and Its Engagement of Scripture* (Grand Rapids: Brazos Press, 2004), pp. 168-75.

Chapter One discusses Augustine, Bishop of Hippo in Northern Africa in the fifth century. Chapter Two describes the practice of Gregory the Great, Bishop of Rome in the late sixth century, the Rule of Saint Benedict, and the practice of Bernard of Clairvaux, the twelfth-century abbot of the Cistercian Order in France. Chapter Three looks at the thirteenth-century Mendicant Orders and their two most significant representatives: Bonaventure of the Franciscans and Thomas Aquinas of the Dominicans. Chapter Four discusses the work of Erasmus and Hugh Latimer in sixteenth-century England, while Chapter Five looks to the continental Reformation, describing the practice of Martin Luther and John Calvin.[29] The conclusion summarizes the contemporary relevance of this conversation and seeks to identify patterns of wisdom and practice that may contribute to preaching in our time.

The purpose of this conversation is not to replicate the ideas, forms, or styles of preachers from the past for application in the present; rather, it is to imitate habits of faithfulness and excellence embodied in their example. By entering into a conversation that is a living tradition, we may ourselves be led to deeper understanding and expressions of "non-identical repetition," a "knowing how" to perform the Word of God in the particular conditions and circumstances of our time.[30] As Stanley Hauerwas notes,

> Such an appeal to the "past" does not mean that Christians will be faithful today by doing what was done in the past, but by attending to how Christians did what they did in the past we hope to know better how to live now. Of course, since we believe in the communion of saints, it is a comfort to know that our past forbearers are present with us.[31]

---

29. In *Remembering the Christian Past*, Robert Wilken writes, "Authority resides in a person who by actions as well as words invites trust and confidence" (p. 174).

30. Stephen E. Fowl writes, "Indeed, the best way to learn the habits of the practically wise is to find appropriate exemplars to imitate. . . . Practical reasoning is the activity of noting similarities and differences between a model and the particular context in which one tries to live in a manner appropriate to that model. What one strives for is non-identical repetition." See his *Engaging Scripture: A Model for Theological Interpretation* (Oxford: Blackwell, 1998), p. 198.

31. Hauerwas, *Dispatches from the Front: Theological Engagements with the Secular* (Durham: Duke University Press, 1994), p. 188.

Preaching in Communion

We may be encouraged to discover that we are not alone in our struggle to read and speak Scripture as a means of knowing, loving, and living faithfully before the Triune God. As God's people we are part of a living tradition, a story extending down to the present and leaning forward into a future that points us toward Home.[32]

32. Fowl, "Introduction," in *The Theological Interpretation of Scripture*, p. xvii; Hauerwas, "Introduction," in *Sanctify Them in Truth*, p. 6.

CHAPTER 1

Augustine of Hippo:
Preaching the Narrative of Salvation

The only thing, though, it [Scripture] ever asserts is catholic faith. . . . It tells the story of things past, foretells things future, points out things present; but all these things are of value for nourishing and fortifying charity or love, and overcoming and extinguishing cupidity or greed.

AUGUSTINE OF HIPPO

Throughout their history Christians have generally read, spoken, and prayed the narrative of Scripture to guide, correct, and edify their faith, worship, and practice as essential aspects of their ongoing struggle to live faithfully before the Triune God.[1] Augustine, Bishop of Hippo (d. A.D. 430), was arguably the most salutary exemplar of narrative reading and preaching during the early centuries of the Western church. As Hans Frei notes, "Long before a minor modern school of thought made the biblical 'history of salvation' a special spiritual and historical sequence for historical and theological inquiry, Christian preachers and theological commentators, Augustine the most notable

1. Stephen Fowl, "Introduction," in *The Theological Interpretation of Scripture: Classic and Contemporary Readings*, ed. Stephen Fowl (Oxford: Oxford University Press, 1997), p. xiii.

Portions of this essay have been previously published in "Narrative Reading, Narrative Preaching: Inhabiting the Story of Scripture," in *Narrative Reading, Narrative Preaching: Reuniting New Testament Interpretation and Christian Proclamation*, ed. Joel B. Green and Michael Pasquarello III (Grand Rapids: Baker Academic Books, 2003).

among them, had envisioned the real world as formed by the sequence told by the biblical stories."[2]

Augustine began with the scriptural word, with the particular story the Bible has to tell, through which the stories of Christian people and the peoples of the world are then told. Because he immersed himself in the world of Scripture, his imagination and life were so shaped by its grand narrative that he struggled to "insert everything from Platonism and the Pelagian problem to the Fall of Rome into the Bible."[3] Because he envisaged Christian doctrine, biblical interpretation, and the practices of the church as constituting a single, coherent world inhabited by Christian people, Augustine serves as a salutary exemplar of theological and pastoral wisdom, whose practice speaks to our contemporary desire for "authentic" preaching and a way to close the gap between "text and sermon."[4]

As bishop of Regius Hippo in Northern Africa, Augustine was confronted by numerous challenges that accompanied the legalization of Christianity by the Roman Empire.[5] He wrote of these conditions, ironically, in a letter: "In this city are many houses in which there is not even a single pagan, nor a single household in which there is not a Christian." Augustine thus preached during a time when the stability of neither Christianity nor the empire was secure. The last twenty years of his life, beginning with the sack of Rome under Alaric in 410, saw the crumbling of the Western empire under the stress of barbarian invasions. His experience of the church, although officially post-Constantinian and with some benefit from government favor, was more that of the *diaspora;* his world was still intellectually and religiously pluralistic.

Augustine's ministry, therefore, was not conducted within an envi-

---

2. Frei, *The Eclipse of Biblical Narrative: A Study in Eighteenth- and Nineteenth-Century Hermeneutics* (New Haven: Yale University Press, 1974), p. 1.

3. George A. Lindbeck, *The Nature of Doctrine: Religion and Theology in a Postliberal Age* (Philadelphia: Westminster Press, 1984), p. 117.

4. For a good introduction to patristic practice, see Christopher A. Hall, *Reading Scripture with the Fathers* (Downers Grove, Ill.: InterVarsity Press, 1998).

5. Here I follow Frederick Van der Meer, *Augustine the Bishop* (London: Sheed & Ward, 1961); Carol Harrison, *Augustine: Christian Truth and Fractured Humanity* (Oxford: Oxford University Press, 2000); Peter Iver Kaufman, *Church, Book, and Bishop: Conflict and Authority in Early Latin Christianity* (Boulder, Colo.: Westview Press, 1996), pp. 75-102; Peter Brown, *Augustine of Hippo: A Biography* (Berkeley and Los Angeles: University of California Press, 1969).

ronment of comfortably established catholic orthodoxy. Fierce competition for the loyalties of his people came from Donatists, who provoked a bitter and even violent schism within the church, and also from the surrounding pagan culture, which, in addition to a variety of religions, philosophies, and folk superstitions, offered numerous enticements in the form of sensual pleasure and frivolous entertainment at the racetrack, the theatre, the fights, and the public baths.[6]

Moving in a direction that runs counter to modern homiletic sensibilities, Augustine perceived that his primary pastoral task was theological in nature: to wean his people from idolatry, to purify their desires, and to establish an alternative culture that was responsive to God by building up the church in love: "For Augustine the performance of scripture in Church is intended by God and empowered by the Holy Spirit to build communal and personal virtue and to accomplish personal salvation. It moves the reader and hearer from idolatrous alienation into the direct presence of the Triune God."[7]

Augustine, moreover, was no stranger to the human struggle with disordered longings and desires. Through a long process of transformation, he learned that human loves can be satisfied only when rightly ordered through participation in the life of the Triune God; it was after a radical conversion from a world centered on himself to a world centered in God that he began to bridge the gap between what he wanted and what God gives, thereby overcoming the distance between the world he claimed as his own and a whole new world given by God.

Augustine begins the *Confessions* with this prayer: "You have made us for yourself, and our heart is restless until it rests in you."[8] Remembering the power of his conversion, Augustine narrated his intellectual and spiritual journey by means of Scripture to offer his story as an act of prayer and loving adoration to the Triune God. After nine books of autobiographical account, Augustine went on to speak about time, memory, and creation, which hold the clue to the whole. He came to understand his own story as a microcosm of the entire story of creation: the fall into the abyss of chaos, and the conversion of the creaturely order to the love of

6. Van der Meer, *Augustine the Bishop*, chapter 3.

7. Telford Work, *Living and Active: Scripture in the Economy of Salvation* (Grand Rapids: Eerdmans, 2002), p. 307.

8. Augustine, *Confessions*, trans. Henry Chadwick (Oxford: Oxford University Press, 1991), 1.1.4; hereafter cited parenthetically in the text as *Confessions*.

God through experiencing the pain of homesickness. Significantly, what the first nine books illustrate in Augustine's personal exploration of the experience of the prodigal son is given cosmic dimension in the concluding parts of the *Confessions*.[9] Christopher Thompson comments,

> The normative guiding principle guiding the *Confessions* is the doctrine of the Church concerning God as the Triune Creator of all that exists and the Redeemer of all who seek reconciliation. . . . The overriding motif of any narrative of Christian experience is the claim that "God has made us for himself." . . . This is the drama of the revelatory narratives: that I find in them not confirmation of myself, but the very constitution of myself. I do not place the actions of God within the horizon of my story; rather, I place my story within the actions of God.[10]

Augustine's new character or identity was constituted by a new narrative: the story of Christ enacted by the common life of the church, which was also the primary context for his vocation as both a reader and a preacher of Scripture. Prior to his conversion he was a highly successful "peddler of words" as a teacher of rhetoric, but now, blessed with the gifts of wisdom and humility, his life was reoriented to become an instrument of loving response to the Word of God spoken in Christ and Scripture. Moreover, the new world he entered through his conversion and incorporation into the church enabled him to make sense of the gap that he perceived as dividing the world of the Bible and the world of history, science, and culture. The relation between Incarnation and rhetoric, the temporal lifeblood of the proclamation of God's Word through preaching, is established from the start.[11]

This new world, however, was not of Augustine's making. Rather, it was created on the basis of the Incarnation, the Word made flesh, and constituted by a particular way of rendering the world — namely, Holy Scripture, a source of continuing delight in its surprising disclosures: "What wonderful profundity there is in your eloquence! The surface

9. Henry Chadwick, *Augustine* (Oxford: Oxford University Press, 1986), pp. 68-70.

10. Thompson, *Christian Doctrine, Christian Identity: Augustine and the Narratives of Character* (Lanham, Md.: University Press of America, 1999), pp. 90-92.

11. Thompson, *Christian Doctrine, Christian Identity*, pp. 78-91; Calvin L. Troup, *Temporality, Eternity, and Wisdom: The Rhetoric of Augustine's "Confessions"* (Columbia: University of South Carolina Press, 1999), pp. 2-5; Work, *Living and Active*, pp. 56-59.

meaning lies open before us and charms beginners. Yet the depth is amazing, my God, the depth is amazing" (*Confessions*, 12.14.17).[12]

Moreover, the language of Incarnation, derived from the whole biblical story of salvation that culminated in Christ, offered Augustine not only a disciplined Way but also a compelling nearness in the Word: the vitality of God's love revealed in Christ had drawn near through the apparent lowliness of the church — in its sacraments, Scripture, sermons, and saints — to overcome his fear of God's persistent call to conversion and a holy life. Scripture became, for Augustine, a sign of the presence of the Lord among his people, a means of continuing the revelation of the incarnate Christ:[13]

> To possess my God, the humble Jesus, I was not yet humble enough. I did not know what his weakness was meant to teach. Your Word, eternal truth, higher than the superior parts of your creation, raises those submissive to him to himself. In the inferior parts he built for himself a humble house of our clay. By this he detaches from themselves those who are willing to be made his subjects and carries them across to himself, healing their swelling and nourishing their love. They are no longer to place their confidence in themselves, but rather to become weak. . . . In their weariness they fall prostrate before this divine weakness which rises and lifts them up. (*Confessions*, 7.18.24)

Soon after his election to the episcopacy, Augustine began to write *De Doctrina Christiana* (*On Christian Doctrine*), the church's first handbook to assist preachers in discovering and communicating divine wisdom for the church's embodiment of the faith and love mediated in the Word of God.[14] Augustine hoped to produce the sort of preachers who would possess the capacity for Christian speech informed by sacred rhetoric, di-

---

12. See William H. Willimon, *Pastor: The Theology and Practice of Ordained Ministry* (Nashville: Abingdon Press, 2002), pp. 199-200.

13. William Mallard, *Language and Love: Introducing Augustine's Religious Thought through the "Confessions" Story* (University Park: Pennsylvania State Press, 1994), pp. 135-36.

14. Augustine, *De Doctrina Christiana*, in *The Works of Augustine: A Translation for the Twenty-First Century*, trans. John E. Rotelle, O.S.A., ed. Edmund Hill, O.P. (Hyde Park, N.Y.: New City Press, 1996): I/II; hereafter cited parenthetically in the text as *DDC*. For an excellent description of Augustine's interpretation of Scripture for preaching, see Karlfried Froehlich, "Take Up and Read: Basics of Augustine's Biblical Interpretation," *Interpretation* 58, no. 1 (January 2004): 5-16, and Rebecca Harden Weaver, "Reading the Signs: Guidance for the Pilgrim Community," *Interpretation* 58, no. 1 (January 2004).

vine eloquence, the Wisdom of Christ spoken in the persuasive power of the Spirit. Moreover, as a newly elected episcopal leader, Augustine needed to establish himself as a reliable interpreter and teacher of Christian doctrine, thereby demonstrating the significant transformation that had taken place in his own life. In Book Four, the conclusion of the work, Augustine summarized his purpose:

> I, for my part, give thanks to our God that in these four books I have set out to the best of my poor ability, not what sort of pastor I am myself, lacking many of the necessary qualities as I do, but what sort the pastor should be who is eager to toil away, not only for his own sake but for others, in the teaching of sound Christian doctrine. (*DDC*, 4.31.64)

The prologue of the work provides a clue for understanding what Augustine means by "what sort the pastor should be." He states that certain rules for dealing with Scripture must be passed on to those who are willing and qualified to learn, since to become a preacher in the church is to be situated within a tradition, the story of a community of interpreters and speakers who have been united by the gift of charity. Indeed, individual inspiration and intelligence or personal creativity and charisma do not rule out the need for preachers to learn from the wisdom of faithful exemplars. The biblical narrative demonstrates how Paul was taught by God, but he was also sent to Ananias to receive the sacraments; the centurion was addressed by an angel, but later he was turned over to Peter; Moses learned from his father-in-law how to govern; Philip explained Isaiah's mysteries to an Ethiopian eunuch (*DDC*, Prologue).

According to Augustine, the most persuasive example is charity, which binds the members of the church one to another as a community of readers and speakers. He asks, "What do we have, after all, that we have not received? But if we have received it, why should we boast as though we had not?" (*DDC*, Prologue). Augustine articulates the significance of this traditioning process in the *Confessions,* praising God for granting both divine and human assistance, for sending preachers who mediated the gift of faith through the ministry of the Word Incarnate, the Son, in the church:

> But no one may call upon God unless God is known, for an ignorant person might call upon someone else. Faith must precede prayer, and faith comes by preaching (Rom. 10:14). You have been preached to us.

My faith, Lord, calls upon you. It is your gift to me. You breathed it into me by the humanity of your Son, by the ministry of your preacher. (*Confessions*, 1.1.5-8)

De Doctrina Christiana is best translated as "Teaching Christianity," thereby taking *doctrina* in the active rather than the passive sense. In writing this book, Augustine is about the business of conversion and Christian formation, revealing his strong commitment to the life-shaping wisdom of Scripture for the church and especially its preachers. Significantly, he begins by offering a vision of the Triune God as the source, means, and goal of all we are, do, and say. Theology and pastoral activity are united, and the preacher's vocation is interpreted within the *ethos* created by the church's received faith and common life in which the vision of love of God and neighbor — the sum of what all Scripture teaches — is attained.[15]

Book One thus introduces a form of spiritual pedagogy that aims to position Augustine's readers within the particular theological world inhabited by the church. It provides a grammar of the rules of Christian faith and conduct shaped around the Creed and embodied in the story of salvation, the way to God through union with Jesus Christ in faith, hope, and love: the doctrine of the Trinity; the Incarnation and mission of Christ; the meaning of Jesus' death and resurrection; the church in pilgrimage; forgiveness of sin; the gift of the Spirit; and the love of God and neighbor to which all Christians are summoned (*DDC*, 1.14.13–20.21).

Because the worship of the Triune God is the ground and enactment of the gift of divine love for the world, it unites Christian people in the enjoyment of God, the Father, through Christ in the fellowship of the church, his body. This fundamental theological conviction enlivens the whole of *De Doctrina Christiana* and informs Augustine's reflection on the reading and preaching of Scripture. Since one must first know the subject matter of Scripture in order to make sense of its words, the fundamental task in learning to read Scripture is the transformation of the preacher, of fitting him or her into the life of God through Christ and the Spirit. One comes to acquire the wisdom of Scripture, the living God, only through a

15. See the excellent discussion of Augustine as theologian and exegete in Frances M. Young, *Biblical Exegesis and the Formation of Christian Culture* (Cambridge: Cambridge University Press, 1997), pp. 265-84.

willingness to be taught and shaped by that reality, the Divine Word, which reveals both the end of human life and the way to this end — communion with God through conformity to Christ.[16]

Moreover, the particular source and goal of this training is the divine wisdom incarnate in Christ, who graciously accommodated himself, reaching out and coming into the world to lead humanity on a journey homeward to God. In Christ, the love of God and the love of neighbor, the "thing" to which all Scripture points, have become one; the humanity of Christ, therefore, leads to the deity of Christ, the indwelling Christ, the indwelling Teacher:[17]

> That is why, since we are meant to enjoy that truth which is unchangeably alive, and since it is in its light that God the Trinity, author and maker of the universe, provides for all the things he has made, our minds have to be purified to enable them to perceive that light, and to cling to it once perceived. We should think of this purification process as being a kind of walk, a kind of voyage to our home country. We do not draw near, after all, by movement in place to the One who is present everywhere, but by honest commitment and good behavior (*DDC*, 1.10.10). . . . Although he is our native country, he made himself also the Way to that country. (*DDC*, 1.11.11)

Pastoral formation occurs by means of contemplation or reverent attention, loving God with the intellect and the will, a way of knowing acquired by constant immersion in Scripture to become participants in its "storied" way of life. This is a sense of theology — *theologia* — that is best defined as a habit of thinking, believing, and acting — *habitus* — a disposition that has the character of personal knowledge of God and the things of God, and which has the character of wisdom — *sapientia* — in relation to the mystery of God. Moreover, the gift of God's illuminating operation of the intellect is directly tied to prayer, virtue, and passionate desire for God.[18]

---

16. Louis Bouyer, *A History of Christian Spirituality*, vol. 1: *The Spirituality of the New Testament and the Fathers* (New York: Seabury Press, 1982), pp. 490-94.

17. Eric O. Springsted, *The Act of Faith: Christian Faith and the Moral Self* (Grand Rapids: Eerdmans, 2002), pp. 130-33.

18. Edward Farley, *Theologia: The Fragmentation and Unity of Theological Education* (Philadelphia: Westminster Press, 1983), pp. 34-35.

Books Two and Three continue Augustine's discussion of interpreting Scripture within the theological "rule" or "grammar" established in Book One: Only the Triune God and the revealed mysteries of faith are to be worshipped and enjoyed for their own sake rather than as commodities to be used; everything else, including biblical exegesis and preaching, must be used wisely to acquire the gifts of faith, hope, and love, thereby promoting a truly Christian way of life in relation to God and others (*DDC*, 1.36.40-44). According to Augustine, Scripture is both magnificent and salutary, adjusted by the Holy Spirit to ward off starvation through the clearer passages and to drive away boredom through the obscure ones. Appropriate reverence toward Scripture prepares for a way of reading that interprets the reader and nurtures humility, a fundamental requirement for true enjoyment and worship of God (*DDC*, 2.7.9–9.14):[19]

> Scripture, though, commands nothing but charity or love, and censures nothing but cupidity, or greed, and that is why it gives shape to human morals. . . . The only thing, though, it ever asserts is catholic faith, with reference to things past and in the future and in the present. It tells the story of things past, foretells things future, points out things present; but all these things are of value for nourishing and fortifying charity or love, and overcoming and extinguishing cupidity or greed. (*DDC*, 3.10.15)

Augustine does not presume that the story or teaching of Scripture is self-evident. Christian doctrine, a grasp of the whole narrative, the economy of creation and redemption constitutes the imaginative world in which Scripture should be read, preached, and lived. "So when, on closer inspection, you see that it is still uncertain how something is to be punctuated or pronounced, you should refer it to the rule of faith, which you have received from the plainer passages and the authority of the church" (*DDC*, 3.2.2). Disciplined study, piety, honesty, courage, self-knowledge, and purity of vision lead to an understanding of what Scripture says and does not say to create the necessary confidence for pastors to speak and congregations to hear God's Word:

19. See the discussion in Frederick Van Fleteren, "Principles of Augustine's Hermeneutic: An Overview," in *Augustine: Biblical Exegete*, ed. Frederick Van Fleteren and Joseph C. Schnaubelt, O.S.A. (New York: Peter Lang, 2001), pp. 1-32.

So these holy people will be so single-minded and pure in heart, that they cannot be diverted from the truth either by any determination to please men, or by a concern to avoid any of those inconveniences that tend to spoil this life. Such children of God are now climbing up to wisdom, which is the last . . . stage, which is to be enjoyed in peace and tranquility. Thus the fear of God, you see, is the beginning of wisdom, and it is through these stages that one moves from that to this. (DDC, 2.7.11)

In addition, certain moral dispositions must be formed, most notably holy fear or reverence before God to heed Scripture's challenge and rebuke, lest anyone thinks he or she knows better than its Divine Author and Speaker. Human complicity in sin and captivity to destructive patterns of living require that pastors must undergo a process of healing and conversion, of unlearning old habits and acquiring new ones fitting for those proficient in Holy Scripture. Christian speech — speaking of God — occurs only when we are personally situated within and transformed by the redeeming, reorienting drama of salvation:

Furthermore, we are still on our way, a way however not from place to place, but one traveled by the affections. And it was being blocked, as by a barricade of thorn bushes, by the malice of our past sins. So what greater generosity and compassion could he show, after deliberately making himself the pavement under our feet along which we could return home, than to forgive us all our sins once we had turned back to him, and by being crucified for us to root out the ban blocking our return that had been so firmly fixed in place? (DDC, 1.17.16)

A strong theology of grace, the divine initiative that underlies Books One through Three, informs Augustine's description of preaching as inspired by the Holy Spirit, the miracle of divine speech that fosters faith through hearing the Word of God. Book Four, which deals with the actual practice of preaching, is less a theory of rhetoric than of conversion, an account of Christian preaching as divine and human activity that transforms by witnessing to the Truth of God discovered in Scripture, which draws the heart and mind to salvation. According to Augustine, God is the Divine Rhetor or Speaker whose wisdom and eloquence, visibly incarnate in Christ, the Mediator, and verbally embodied in sacred

Scripture, are both the message and means of the journey to humanity's heavenly homeland.[20]

Moreover, this homeward journey is "traveled by the affections" as the heart's loves or persuasions are reordered by the persuasiveness of the Word through the language of Scripture. As an expert in the art of rhetoric, a master wordsmith, Augustine was well-acquainted with the enchanting power of human speech. The *Confessions* testifies to his excessive pride and vanity, to the self-absorbed and self-serving ways of his old life prior to his new life in Christ. As he writes, "In all innocence I taught my pupils crafty tricks, not to enable them to secure the death of an innocent man, but on occasion to acquit a guilty one" (*Confessions*, 4.2.2).

Drawing from this experience, Augustine warns that rhetoric must be seen for what it is: a technology of words, an art or technique that can be utilized for either good or ill. In fact, a combination of persuasive power and moral indifference can make rhetoric a dangerous tool, especially in the church; preaching that aims for rhetorical effectiveness can easily follow the drift of popular art forms to become little more than mere entertainment. Shorn of depth of character, habits, and wisdom created by careful, loving attention to the God who is praised in the church's liturgy and expressed in the signs of Scripture, preachers can easily accommodate the Gospel to the pleasure of their listeners.[21]

Augustine does not neglect the need for pastors to acquire a working knowledge of history and biblical languages, or literary and rhetorical skills for the tasks of exegesis and preaching. However, these are subordinated to the practice of indwelling the world of Scripture and cultivating a love of truth that enables one to acquire particular habits of believing, thinking, and speaking. Furthermore, Augustine's continued interest in rhetoric must be seen in light of his desire to describe preaching as a practice informed and inspired by the truth of Scripture, its rhetorical eloquence and beauty that instructs, delights, and persuades the heart and mind toward love of God and neighbor. Paradoxically, preaching proceeds by means of a "studied neglect" in its use of the rhetorical arts,

20. John C. Cavadini, "The Sweetness of the Word: Salvation and Rhetoric in Augustine's *De Doctrina Christiana*," in *De Doctrina Christiana: A Classic of Western Culture*, ed. Duane W. H. Arnold and Pamela Bright (Notre Dame: University of Notre Dame Press, 1995), pp. 166-68.

21. William Harmless, S.J., *Augustine and the Catechumenate* (Collegeville, Minn.: Liturgical Press, 1995), pp. 357-59.

since wisdom and eloquence are cultivated by careful attention to the language and style of Scripture, which is sacramental, the inspired word of God.[22] Such disciplined reading fosters flexibility and freedom in crafting homiletic form and style, an art best learned by imitating salutary exemplars:

> The fact is, given a bright and eager disposition, eloquence will come more readily to those who read and listen to eloquent speakers than those who pore over the rules of eloquence. Nor is there any lack of ecclesiastical writers, over and above the canon of scripture that has been set for our salvation at the summit of authority, by whose style a capable man will be influenced when he reads them, even if that is not his concern, but he is only interested in what they have to say; and he will put this to good use when he has occasion to write or dictate, or finally even to preach what he has in mind that accords with the piety and rule of faith. (*DDC*, 4.3.4)

Delight in the artistry of the preacher or the literary forms of Scripture creates a love that signals beyond them to their inspiration and source: the love of God. Thus the formation of Christian speech that draws and moves the church to hear and obey the Word requires knowledge and understanding that transcends but does not exclude the art of rhetoric. Most important is the need for preachers to acquire a sense of knowing how to speak in the midst of changing capacities, conditions, and circumstances. Such knowledge requires that the preacher be shaped not only by disciplined study but even more by devotion and prayer, assimilated to Christ and his wisdom to become an example of living interpretation — an "eloquent sermon" (*DDC*, 4.29.62). Augustine observes,

> They should familiarize themselves with the kinds of expression in the Holy Scriptures and be on alert to observe how things are commonly said in them, and to commit them to memory. But much more impor-

---

22. Carol Harrison, "The Rhetoric of Scripture and Preaching: Classical Decadence or Christian Aesthetic?" in *Augustine and His Critics: Essays in Honour of Gerald Bonner*, ed. Robert Dodaro and George Lawless (London and New York: Routledge, 2000), pp. 221-25; Luke Timothy Johnson, "Augustine and the Demands of Charity," in *The Future of Catholic Biblical Scholarship: A Constructive Conversation*, ed. Luke Timothy Johnson and William S. Kurz, S.J. (Grand Rapids: Eerdmans, 2002), pp. 116-17; Robert Louis Wilken, *The Spirit of Early Christian Thought: Seeking the Face of God* (New Haven: Yale University Press, 2003), pp. 76-78.

tant than that, and supremely necessary, is that they should pray for understanding. After all, in this very literature, which they are eager to study, they read that the Lord gives wisdom and from his face comes knowledge and understanding. (*DDC*, 3.37.56)

Performing Scripture

In his preaching Augustine attributed special status to Christian revelation, the Word of God speaking through Scripture and human speech to God's people, *verbum dei* in *sermo dei*, thus mediating the truth of God's dramatic activity of salvation to the understanding, heart, and will.[23] With his use of the Bible, Augustine aimed to form Christians into a holy people, speaking a common language and way of life that was to be received and shared.[24] By trusting the language of Scripture and the work of the Holy Spirit to inform and empower his speech, Augustine subordinated his words to Christ, the living Word, who instructs, delights, and transforms listeners.

Augustine delivered most of his sermons to popular audiences, not primarily the educated, and he always aimed to give a clear exposition of the biblical text. For a good example consider the more than 120 sermons, or tractates, from the Gospel of John, which are characterized by clarity, orthodox teaching, and pastoral wisdom. Augustine preached these sermons extemporaneously, exercising discipline and flexibility, adhering to the text while remaining attuned to the capacities of his congregation. In this preaching the drama was salvation, its script was Scripture, and its actors included everyone.[25] Frederick Van der Meer describes Augustine's congregational cast:

> There, then, stand the people of Hippo, fishermen, sailors, business folk and strangers who are passing through. . . . Right in front are the children. . . . At a place set apart are the dedicated virgins and widows

23. See Harrison, "The Rhetoric of Scripture and Preaching," pp. 214-30. See also the excellent description in Brown, *Augustine of Hippo*, pp. 250-58.

24. See the discussion of the use of the Bible in the early church in Wilken, *The Spirit of Early Christian Thought*, pp. 50-79.

25. Harmless, *Augustine and the Catechumenate*, pp. 235, 346-82; Van der Meer, *Augustine the Bishop*, pp. 405-12.

in their dark veils, the penitents and catechumens being similarly cut off from the rest. The *curiales* of the city have taken their places right in front, as have the commandment of the coastal guard and the other notables. These people's children are in the care of slaves, waiting-women looking after the girls, while the boys are in the charge of "pedagogues." Last, there is a great crowd of Berbers, mixed with the scum of a Mediterranean port; they are an evil-smelling lot, though picturesquely decked out.[26]

Augustine had his pastoral work cut out for him in shaping this diverse collection of individuals and groups into a Christian community that in its common life would bear faithful witness to the Gospel. George Lindbeck has persuasively argued that it was Scripture, the basic Christian Bible, that had the consensus-, community-, and institution-building power to make of these diverse peoples the overwhelmingly dominant and therefore Catholic Church. Moreover, "this community-forming role was instrumental in constituting the *ecclesia* only when interpreted communally in accordance with a community-constituting hermeneutics."[27]

In 407 Augustine began to deliver the aforementioned series of homilies on the Gospel of John with the intention of expounding the book from beginning to end. With the arrival of Eastertide, however, he interrupted this series, since the scriptural readings for Holy Week and for the Octave of Easter were fixed to some extent. It was also the custom during the Easter Octave to have both a morning liturgy and an evening liturgy every day. And those newly baptized on the Easter Vigil would attend the evening service dressed in white and gathered together in a special section apart from the others in attendance. It was appropriate that the sermons at this time be especially relevant to the spiritual needs of those neophyte Christians who had just been transferred through the act of baptism from a world of darkness into the glorious light and life of the Risen Christ and his body, the church.[28]

What to preach? How to preach? These were questions that Augus-

---

26. Van der Meer, *Augustine the Bishop*, pp. 389-90.

27. George Lindbeck, "Scripture, Consensus, and Community," in *Biblical Interpretation in Crisis: The Ratzinger Conference on Bible and Church*, ed. Richard John Neuhaus (Grand Rapids: Eerdmans, 1989), pp. 78-80.

28. Hughes Oliphant Old, *The Reading and Preaching of the Scriptures in the Worship of the Christian Church*, vol. 2: *The Patristic Age* (Grand Rapids: Eerdmans, 1998), pp. 344-68.

tine, like any other preacher, presumably must have pondered. He chose in this particular year the First Epistle of John.[29] The epistle was short, and he expected to complete its exposition during the Easter Octave. But there were other reasons for this choice: Augustine considered it the work of the Apostle John, who, he believed, also wrote the Fourth Gospel. He therefore made this announcement to his congregation:

> We shall then still be listening to him whose Gospel we have for a while put down. It is a book very sweet to every healthy Christian heart that savours the bread of God; and it should be constantly in the mind of God's Holy Church. But I chose it more particularly because what it specially means to us is charity. The man who has in himself that of which he hears must rejoice at the hearing. To him this reading will be like oil on the flame: if there is matter in him for nourishment, it will be nourished; it will grow and abide. For some the Epistle should be like flame to firewood: if it was not already burning, the touch of the wind may kindle it. In some, then, what is present is to be nourished; in some what may be lacking is to be kindled; so that we may all rejoice in one single charity. . . . Where there is humility, there is charity. (*Ten Homilies*, 259-60)

Because Augustine was less preoccupied with the world that produced the Bible and more concerned with learning to live in the world that Scripture produces, he viewed his listeners as members of a community created by the Risen Christ, who continues to address his church through the apostolic witness. Augustine perceived that charity, manifested in the humility of Christ, was the primary focus and force of John's First Epistle, a topic as relevant to his North African church as when the epistle was first written. Augustine was also convinced that *caritas* (charity, or love of God and others that leads to holiness and happiness) was the foundation of the church's life, and thereby instruction in it was fitting for new Christians and beneficial for experienced ones. And then too, in spite of recent legislation whereby the Roman government had condemned the Donatist schism, the church at Hippo remained divided, and Catholic Christians and Donatist Christians persisted in their hatred

---

29. Augustine, *Ten Homilies on the First Epistle of St. John*, trans. John Burnaby, Library of Christian Classics (Philadelphia: Westminster Press, 1955), pp. 251-348; hereafter cited parenthetically in the text as *Ten Homilies*.

for one another. Augustine considered it most appropriate to preach on divine love as the source and goal of Christian unity. Love could heal the schism, unify the church of Hippo, and purify the hearts of all Christians, both young and old in the faith.[30]

For Augustine, the preaching of the Word of God found in Scripture constituted and nurtured the church in union with Christ, its Head. At the same time, the church, joined to Christ, was incorporated into the Word, which it read and heard in its liturgical gatherings. At least this was Augustine's hope, which he announced at the beginning of the first homily on 1 John 1:1:

> One might understand "the word of life" as a speaking about Christ, and the actual body of Christ, handled with hands. But see what follows: "and the life itself was manifested." Christ, then, is the word of life. . . . The life itself has been manifested in the flesh — set in manifestation, that the eyes, for the healing of hearts, might see what the heart alone can see. Only by the heart is the Word seen; flesh is seen by bodily eyes. We had the means of seeing the Word: the Word was made flesh, which we could see, that the heart, by which we should see the Word, might be healed. (*Ten Homilies*, 260-61)

Moreover, the goal of the entire sweep of salvation — "the Word became flesh and dwelt among us" — is fulfilled when that flesh is joined to the church, which is the whole Christ — *totus Christus* — Head and Body:[31]

> It is we who are so described and designated. Let us then receive the blessing which the Lord has promised; let us hold fast that which we see not, since they who saw have made it known to us. . . . You may think it no great matter to have fellowship with men, but see what follows: "and our fellowship be with God the Father and his Son, Jesus Christ." "These things we write to you that your joy may be full." That fullness of joy is in the fellowship, the charity, the unity itself. (*Ten Homilies*, 263)

---

30. I am indebted to the discussion of these homilies by Lewis Ayres, "Augustine on God as Love and Love as God," *Pro Ecclesia* 5, no. 4 (Fall 1996): 470-87.

31. For Augustine's exposition of the *totus Christus*, see *De Doctrina Christiana*, 3.30.42ff. See also the discussion by Young, *Biblical Exegesis and the Formation of Christian Culture*, pp. 282-84.

This was Augustine's message of Easter joy and hope to his people. "Listen: there may be a word of comfort, encouragement, and hope that we faint not by the way. We are fellow travelers, traveling to our homeland, and if we despair of reaching it, in our despair we faint. But he whose will it is that we should reach the homeland where he will keep us, nourishes us upon our journey" (*Ten Homilies*, 264). Thus the story of Jesus Christ is the Triune God's humble doorway to time and time's doorway to the Trinitarian life of God. "Easter is the good news of the Father, who, through the Son and in the Spirit, enters into relationship with human history so that humanity may reach and enter into the very life of the Trinity."[32]

Augustine thus rendered the witness of John as a compelling invitation to his people to indwell the world of Scripture — not as encouragement to focus on the Bible in itself, but as a persuasive summons into the narrative of salvation, a journey beginning and ending in God, but yet to be consummated by the transforming power of divine love mediated through the missions of the Son and the Spirit within and for the whole Christian community.[33] "By love," Augustine continued,

> the heart's eye must continually be cleansed and strengthened for the sight of that changeless Being, in whose presence the lover may ever delight, and enjoy it in the society of angels unto all eternity. But now we must run his course, so that one day he may rejoice in his true fatherland. . . . Let us never go back on our journeying: let us hold to the Church's unity, hold to Christ, hold to charity. . . . That this is the end, for which and unto which we run our course: when we reach it we shall have rest (*Ten Homilies*, 337).

Because Christ is the culmination of God's self-communication, Augustine viewed the wholeness of Christ's work, his condescension to humanity, as including the life of the church and its Scripture. Moreover, since Christ epitomizes the rule for the church's reading of Scripture — he is the Word behind its words — Christ is given in the church's reading of

---

32. Bruno Forte, *The Trinity as History: Saga of the Christian God*, trans. Paul Rotondi, O.F.M. (New York: Alba House, 1989), p. 53.

33. I am following Ayres's excellent discussion of charity, community, and the Trinity in Augustine's homilies on 1 John, "Augustine on God as Love and Love as God," pp. 470-78.

the text: it is a sacrament of his presence. Through the Spirit's work, Christ, the Word of God, is manifested in the flesh when Scripture is rehearsed and performed by the whole church in the unity of charity, the fellowship of Triune love.[34] This theological perspective, shaped by the Rule of Faith, was central for Augustine's exposition of 1 John: "So, my brothers, let us make haste and love the Christ. That Christ is Jesus: and who is he? The Word of God; the manner of his coming to our sick world is that 'the Word became flesh and dwelt among us'" (*Ten Homilies*, 344-45).

Peter Brown has written of the manner in which bishops like Augustine presented Christianity to the ancient world, offering a universal way of salvation that was gathering all nations and all classes into its bosom, *populari sinu*. The Bible itself, with its layers of meaning, was a microcosm, a textual world, of the social and intellectual diversity to be found in Christian churches, so that the humblest of the earth should be drawn, moved, and at home in them. As Augustine acknowledged in the *Confessions*,

> I now began to believe that you would never have conferred such preeminent authority on the scripture, now diffused through all lands, unless you had willed that it would be a means of coming to faith in you, and a means of seeking to know you. . . . The authority of the Bible seemed the more venerated and more worthy of a holy faith on the ground that it was open to everyone to read. . . . The Bible offered itself to all in very accessible words and the most humble style of diction. . . . It welcomes all people to its generous embrace, and also brings a few to you through narrow openings. Though the latter are few, they are much more numerous than would be the case if the Bible did not stand out by its high authority and if it had not drawn crowds to the bosom of its holy humility. (*Confessions*, 6.5.8)[35]

Augustine viewed the Incarnation as the highest example of divine grace without regard to human merit; he held that humanity is incapable of itself of participating in God, and can hope to do so only as a member of Christ's Body, the church. It was from within this participation, which itself was a gift of grace that Augustine preached, that anyone, regardless

---

34. Springsted, *The Act of Faith*, pp. 133-47; Mallard, *Language and Love*, pp. 161-64.

35. See the discussion in Peter Brown, *Power and Persuasion in Late Antiquity* (Madison: University of Wisconsin Press, 1988), pp. 74-75.

of station in life, might participate in the divine. Thus the language and style of both Scripture and the speakers it produced formed the basis of a Christian populism, *sermo humilis:* humble speech endowed with divine charity to address both the "high and low" of the empire.[36] The diversity of Christian congregations, the simplicity of Christian scriptures, the lack of cultural status of many Christian heroes, the Christian care of the poor and disenfranchised — all these things lent a sense of concreteness to the grand outlines within the Christian imagination that envisaged a church empowered by God's providence, a narrative capable of absorbing all levels of Roman society. Commenting on Augustine's homilies on 1 John, Lewis Ayres writes,

> Augustine's theological departure . . . is our participation in the mystery of Easter, the participation of the contemporary Christian community in the saving events of God's redemptive dispensation. On this basis he is able to build up a profoundly Trinitarian theology which is also a theology attentive to the process of actual Christian life and formation, attentive to the central place of our created temporal existence as a gift of God, a gift enabling our sharing in God . . . which only makes sense within the slow process of coming to realize that the One who is love has revealed himself and inaugurated a practice of formed love and confession through which we may share in the Triune life of love itself.[37]

Christian gestures of compassion to the poor, therefore, emphasized a basic level of human solidarity, just as God, in the person of Christ, freely identified himself with human flesh, becoming a fellow son of the earth, a kinsman of the human race.[38] The appeal of Christianity lay in its radical sense of community; it absorbed people because the individual could drop from a wide, impersonal world into a miniature community whose demands and relations were explicit.[39] Averil Cameron observes,

---

36. Averil Cameron, *Christianity and the Rhetoric of Empire: The Development of Christian Discourse* (Berkeley and Los Angeles: University of California Press, 1991), pp. 111-12.

37. Ayres, "Augustine on God as Love and Love as God," p. 478.

38. Brown, *Power and Persuasion in Late Antiquity*, pp. 76, 153; Brown, *Authority and the Sacred: Aspects of the Christianization of the Roman World* (Cambridge: Cambridge University Press, 1995), pp. 10-11.

39. Peter Brown, *The World of Late Antiquity* (London: Thames & Hudson, 1971), p. 76.

"Out of the framework of Judaism, and living as they did in the Roman Empire and in the context of Greek philosophy, pagan practice, and contemporary social ideas, Christians built themselves a new world."[40]

On Continuing the Story

Augustine's grand narration of the Christian story, *The City of God*, which he wrote in response to the pastoral problems facing the church of his day, identified the church as a pilgrim people — ruled by Christ, the Crucified Lord, and devoted to the Triune God — on a journey, a "theo-drama" through time toward their destiny in the heavenly city.[41] Augustine writes of the path, or the Way, Christ made known through Scripture and God stretched out between humanity and its final goal — perfection in love of God and neighbor as accomplished by the Incarnation:

> If there is no path, or if a man does not know which way to go, there is little use in knowing the destination. As it is, there is one road, and one only, well secured against all of going astray; and this road is provided by one who himself is God and man. As God, he is the goal; as man, he is the way. This Mediator spoke in former times through the Prophets and later through his own mouth, and after that through the apostles, telling all that he decided was enough for man. He also instituted the Scripture, those that we call canonical.[42]

In contrast to the city of God, Augustine depicted the earthly city as a community constituted by self-love to the point of contempt for God; its glory is in itself, its wisdom, and its strength. By reading the world through the lens of the biblical story, Augustine came to understand history as an open-ended narrative involving two cities and their opposing ways of life based on either love of God or love of domination.

The church in history remains a thoroughly mixed body, ever engaging in a dramatic struggle with questions regarding who we are and whose we are until attaining the eschatological peace of the heavenly

---

40. Cameron, *Christianity and the Rhetoric of Empire*, p. 21.

41. Augustine, *City of God*, ed. David Knowles, trans. Henry Bettenson (New York: Pelican Books, 1972).

42. Augustine, *City of God*, 11.2-3.

city.[43] As Augustine noted, "The Church proceeds on its pilgrim way in this world, in these evil days. Its troubled course began . . . with Abel himself . . . and the pilgrimage goes on right up to the end of history."[44] His book is a defense of the worship of the one true God, the God who was acknowledged in ancient Israel, revealed in Christ, and venerated in the church. Yet this God has no life independent of the practice of Christian people, of those who know God in prayer and devotion, those who belong to a community of memory and are bound together in common service, comprising a society of aliens, or strangers, in this world.[45]

Thus in a world of competing and often violent interests, the most faithful service the church can render is to embody the weakness and humility of its crucified Lord, thereby disclosing a fundamental truth about human beings and society: without true worship and love for God, there can be no human fulfillment, happiness, or genuine communal life. To paraphrase Augustine, we are made in the image of God, and we are restless until we find rest — peace — in God.[46] Augustine observes,

> Justice is found where God . . . rules an obedient city to his grace . . . so that just as the individual righteous man lives on the basis of faith which is active in love, so the association, or people, of righteous men lives on the same basis of faith, active in love, the love with which a man loves God as God ought to be loved, and loves his neighbor as himself. But where this justice does not exist, there is certainly no "association of men united by a common sense of right and by a community of interest."[47]

The formation of ecclesial identity, God's pilgrim people called out from all nations, required that Christian liturgical gatherings be characterized by attentive, reverent receptivity and enactment of the biblical

43. See the discussion of Augustine's ecclesiology in Nicholas M. Healy, *Church, World, and the Christian Life: Practical-Prophetic Life* (Cambridge: Cambridge University Press, 2000), pp. 54-56.

44. Augustine, *City of God*, 15.1, p. 597.

45. Robert L. Wilken, *Remembering the Christian Past* (Grand Rapids: Eerdmans, 1995), pp. 60-61.

46. Robert L. Wilken, "Augustine's City of God Today," in *The Two Cities of God: The Church's Responsibility for the Earthly City*, ed. Carl E. Braaten and Robert W. Jenson (Grand Rapids: Eerdmans, 1997), pp. 28-31; Wilken, *The Spirit of Early Christian Thought*, pp. 186-211.

47. Augustine, *City of God*, 19.23.

script, a communal sacrifice of praise to the Triune God, whose love creates, redeems, and perfects all that is. In Augustine's vision, "going to church" is a journey to the place where Christian people behold their destiny, where they see what is to become of them, where they are formed into a people of hope. The church's primary task is to become what it is: the embodiment of God's salvation revealed in Christ and declared through Holy Scripture.[48]

Preaching as a Theological and Pastoral Practice

A salutary exemplar of preaching as a theological and pastoral practice, Augustine read the narrative of salvation as the center of Scripture: the single great book in which God speaks of himself and humanity, the gift of salvation realized in the fullness of love for God and neighbor. When Augustine proclaimed the Gospel, it was as if Christ was truly present among his people, speaking to them personally through Scripture, sermon, and sacrament, the one Word sounding through the many words of the prophets, apostles, and saints.[49]

Furthermore, the wonder is this: God's story and the human story give us not two interwoven books, one human, one divine, which we can divide at will, but one indivisible book, one Bible. Augustine heard God "speaking not only in the grand moments but also in the everyday human flaws and failings in the telling of the human story; he recognized that the exalted passages are not only divine but still fully and truly human. The two stories, God's and our own, are both fully present in each part of the one, single story we call the Bible."[50]

---

48. Jenson, "How the World Lost Its Story," in *The New Religious Humanists: A Reader*, ed. Gregory Wolfe (New York: Free Press, 1997), p. 147; Stanley M. Hauerwas, *After Christendom: How the Church Is to Behave if Freedom, Justice, and a Christian Nation Are Bad Ideas* (Nashville: Abingdon Press, 1991), p. 44.

49. John Norris, "Augustine and Sign in *Tractatus in Johannis Euangelium*," in *Augustine: Biblical Exegete*, ed. Van Fleteren and Schnaubelt, pp. 218-22.

50. James William McClendon Jr., *Systematic Theology: Doctrine* (Nashville: Abingdon Press, 1994), pp. 275-76.

CHAPTER 2

Monastic Voices
in the Story of Sacred Rhetoric

The monastic tradition is a rich source of theological and pastoral wisdom united within the spiritual life: love of God and love of neighbor as articulated in Scripture and the Fathers. From Christian antiquity to the thirteenth century and the birth of the universities, monasteries were the church's primary centers of learning, of devotion to God through both mind and heart, worship and work, prayer and preaching.

In this chapter I want to focus on three outstanding figures. I will begin with Gregory the Great, a significant monastic exemplar of both the contemplative and the active life. He was a pastor whose preaching was the fruit of prayerful study of God, and whose vocation of speaking and writing was done in service to the church in sixth-century Rome, over which he was appointed to rule as its chief shepherd. I will then discuss St. Benedict, author of the most influential expression of monastic wisdom: the Rule of St. Benedict. It offers a particular vision of how one's mind, will, speech, and action must be disciplined and ordered to the praise of God. Finally, I will explore the vocation of Bernard of Clairvaux, arguably the most outstanding monastic preacher of the medieval period. In him and his work we see the fruit of the spiritual life, a way of thinking and speaking shaped by biblical and patristic wisdom that flowed freely from and for the love of God.

Gregory the Great: Pastoral Theologian

Gregory I, Bishop of Rome during the latter half of the sixth century (d. 604), was pressed into pastoral ministry during a time of calamity, when the "end of the world" — both a tradition and the local world — daily seemed at hand. Although fourteen hundred years separate us from the world of Gregory the Great, we who live during a time of significant changes in the life of the church and surrounding culture may learn from the exemplary character, moral passion, and practical wisdom of one who reluctantly left behind a peaceable monastic life to "steer into port the old and rotten ship of which, in the hidden dispensation of God, I have assumed the guidance."[1]

Gregory's times were made of "the stuff of apocalyptic dreams and visions." The last Western Roman emperor was deposed in 476, replaced by German kings who were unable to remedy the structural weakness of the Italian economy: a shortage of manpower, high taxes, and low productivity thwarted capital formation. And in 535 the Emperor Justinian sent out forces to reconquer the West, pulling Italy into wars of varying intensity for almost two decades, which brought about unparalleled destruction. Rome was besieged several times; starvation and the plague were widespread; the population dwindled as serious economic recession continued. In 568 the fierce Lombard tribe crossed the Alps, disrupting many episcopal sees and, as memories of Rome's past glory faded, setting up politics in Italy as an ongoing affair between the Lombards, the papacy, and the East.

The earliest years of Gregory's life coincided with Italy's crumbling conditions and instability. Born into a noble and wealthy family, he presumably received the best available education in sixth-century Rome, studying grammar, rhetoric, and dialectic, and probably law as well. He began his religious life in a monastic community he helped to found; he gave away his personal wealth to the poor and served as abbot to the monastery. By Gregory's own admission, these were the happiest years of his life. But in 579 he was called to serve the church in the world as papal legate to Constantinople for Pope Pelagius II. He returned to Rome during the next decade to serve as a deacon of the city, a position of signifi-

---

1. Gregory the Great, *Epistle XLIII*, in *Nicene and Post-Nicene Fathers*, ed. Philip Schaff and Henry Wace, vol. 12, 2d series (Peabody, Mass.: Hendrickson Publishers, 1994), p. 87.

cant responsibility, and in 590 he was elected pope, the office he held until his death in 604.[2]

Gregory and the Pastoral Office

As pope, Gregory attempted to accommodate the church to service in the world, but at the same time he hoped to purify the church from secular corruption. When the papacy was forced by Italy's declining social conditions to assume greater responsibility in the secular realm — maintaining supplies of food and water, paying soldiers, negotiating treaties, administering estates, and systematizing charitable operations — Gregory sought to preserve the church from the pollution of secular wisdom. Thus a constant struggle was to characterize Gregory's papacy: the struggle to maintain balance between the contemplative life of the ascetic, one who prays, desiring to know and love God, and the active life of the pastor who shepherds the flock of Christ's people on pilgrimage in and through the world.[3]

Gregory was well read in the Christian tradition, becoming particularly familiar with the works of John Cassian, Cassiodorus, Cyprian, Ambrose, several of the Eastern Fathers, and — most important — Augustine. Yet Gregory's world was very different from the one inhabited by Augustine. As Robert Markus suggests, in Augustine's time the most haunting question was "What is a Christian, and what distinguishes Christian people from their non-Christian neighbors?" On the other hand, Gregory lived in a time when everyone, for practical purposes, was Christian to some degree. He thus preached to convert a church already established in the Christian faith, yet constantly tossed about by the "billows of the world." The questions he presumed to address will be familiar to those who have assumed, at some level, the continuing influence of Christianity in the world: How to be Christian? How to go on to live the

2. Carol Straw, *Gregory the Great: Perfection in Imperfection* (Berkeley and Los Angeles: University of California Press, 1988), pp. 1-27; Robert Markus, *Gregory the Great and His World* (Cambridge: Cambridge University Press, 1997), pp. 1-17; Bernard McGinn, *The Presence of God: A History of Western Mysticism*, 4 vols. (New York: Crossroad, 1991-), vol. 2, pp. 34-79.

3. See the essay on Gregory's spirituality by Dom Jean Leclercq, "From St. Gregory to St. Bernard," in *A History of Christian Spirituality*, vol. 2: *The Spirituality of the Middle Ages*, ed. Jean Leclercq, Francois Vandenbroucke, and Louis Bouyer (New York: Seabury Press, 1982), pp. 3-30.

fullest Christian life? How to remain faithful to God in a time when wars and rumors of wars, social chaos, and economic uncertainty continue to challenge and even shake settled, comfortable forms of faith?[4]

In the months following his election to office, as Gregory continued to struggle with the tension between life in the cloister and immersion in ecclesial affairs, he was helped by his work of systematically reflecting on the themes of the pastoral office, the responsibility of preaching and caring for the church as Christ's flock. Composing the *Regula pastoralis* (*Pastoral Rule*, sometimes translated *Pastoral Care*), a handbook for ecclesial leaders that essentially defined his ministry, became the therapy, the clarifying exercise that reconciled him to the pastoral office, and the profession of faith for the new way of life he would follow. Contemplation — a desire, love, and attentive regard for God — was to be considered within the pastor's function in the Christian community, and conversely, the pastoral ministry itself must have a radically contemplative direction.[5]

The conflict between Gregory's "love for eternity" and his desire to be useful for God's purposes in the church was resolved by the virtue of humility and self-knowledge, *consideratio* (consideration). Governance, or care of souls, teaching and guiding the church, requires a life of moral rectitude; in teaching others to know Christ and aspire to a life of holiness, a pastor must be vigilant in daily recognizing his or her own weaknesses. The danger is that he or she would presume to preach without wisdom, to assume authority for speaking what has not yet been absorbed into his or her life; thus in vanity, says Gregory, "the tongue purveys mere jargon when one thing is learned and another taught" (*PC*, 22). Outward authority, therefore, must be balanced by inner virtue; theological understanding must be joined to spiritual discipline to shape one's Christian insight and experience.

Some are unfit for pastoral office since, while they may know the language of faith, they do not understand its grammar; they do not know how Christian speech works to create and sustain the life of faith. They are like physicians ignorant of the power of the medicine they prescribe,

---

4. Markus, *Gregory the Great and His World*, pp. 23-26, 40-41.

5. St. Gregory the Great, *Pastoral Care*, trans. Henry Davis, S.J., Ancient Christian Writers, no. 11 (New York: Newman Press, 1978); hereafter cited parenthetically in the text as *PC*. I am following the discussion of Markus, *Gregory the Great and His World*, pp. 10-33. See also G. R. Evans, *The Thought of Gregory the Great* (Cambridge: Cambridge University Press, 1986), pp. 17-26, 105-12; McGinn, *The Presence of God*, vol. 2, pp. 38-50.

or shepherds who lead their flocks into dangerous places. Unable to function as dependable guides, as the "eyes" of the church, they are like the blind leading the blind. Christ, therefore, is Gregory's primary model for pastoral ministry, since the Incarnation exemplifies the ecclesial principle that enlivens the *Pastoral Rule:* "Indeed, what disposition of mind is revealed in him, who could perform conspicuous public benefit on coming to his task, but prefers his own privacy to the benefit of others, seeing that the Only-Begotten of the Supreme Father came forth from the bosom of the Father into our midst, that He might benefit many?" (*PC*, 31).

Isaiah, Jeremiah, and Moses offer vivid display of the virtue of humble obedience required for pastoral ministry. Gregory observes that all three were faithful, though in varying ways. Isaiah, who wished to be sent, was cleansed by God; Jeremiah protested his call but was cleansed by supernal or heavenly graces, and therefore he did not resist. However, it was Moses who was humble and obedient in both respects, since in both his unwillingness to be sent to rule over God's people and in his consent to go, he relied on the power of the One who commands. Drawing from the example of Christ and these three Old Testament saints, Gregory describes the manner in which pastors must die to the desires of the flesh: putting aside worldly prosperity, fearing no adversaries, seeking only what nourishes knowledge of God, coveting nothing possessed by others, giving freely to those in need, inclining to be merciful, not sinning by excess, having compassion on others and grieving for their sins, interceding on their behalf, yet striving to please God rather than people (*PC*, 32-34). While pastors must be capable of speaking to water-parched hearts, example always speaks louder than words. As Augustine advised in *De Doctrina Christiana,* preachers must become a "living sermon."

Pastors, however, must be as careful with their words as their behavior, being neither unreasonably silent nor uncautiously verbose. Teachers are called prophets in Sacred Scripture because they oppose worldly enemies with their candid speech, defend the flock with the Truth, and build a wall around the household of God with their words. Gregory thus asks, "If, then, the priest does not know how to preach, what vocal sound is this mute herald to give? For hence it is that the Holy Spirit sat upon the first pastors under the appearance of tongues (Acts 2:3); because whomsoever He has filled, He himself at once makes eloquent" (*PC*, 51-55).

Pastoral discourse must not be hastily given, poorly prepared, or disordered so as to wound hearers with errors and thus sever the bonds that unite the church. Moreover, pastors must not speak in excess or in a slovenly manner; for if loquacity, no matter how admirable, fails to notice practical need, its force is wasted. Preachers are simply called to sow the Word, since it is the seed of their words and the reception of their thoughts as derived from Scripture that shape the minds of hearers. Pastoral care requires prudence or practical wisdom

> to reveal the glory of our homeland in Heaven by preaching, to show what great temptations of the ancient Enemy are lurking in this life's journey, and to correct with severe and zealous asperity those evils in his subjects which cannot be treated with forbearance, lest, being too little incensed against such faults, he himself be held guilty of all.

Such insightfulness, self-knowledge, and charity are acquired only through daily meditation on Scripture, the Sacred Word that admonishes, purifies, and restores; preachers are equipped by "the instruction of the sacred volumes" (*PC*, 86-88).

Formed by Scripture into a certain kind of person, a pastor must possess the judgment to speak the Word to people in all conditions, since what is profitable to some may actually be harmful to others. Herbs that nourish some animals kill others; medicine that alleviates one disease aggravates another; bread may strengthen the life of robust adults but destroy that of little children. As Gregory points out, the prudent pastor must be like a musician who brings forth harmonious sounds from the diversity of characters, conditions, and circumstances that constitute the church: "For what are the minds of attentive hearers but, if I may say so, the taut strings of a harp, which the skillful harpist plays with a variety of strokes, that he may not produce a discordant melody, because they are not plucked with the same kind of stroke, though plucked with the same plectrum" (*PC*, 89-90).

The challenge of preaching, therefore, is to build up the whole church in the one virtue of charity, love for God and love for neighbor, to guide each member with the same doctrine while addressing a wide range of needs. Rather than prescribing a general theory of preaching, Gregory describes the use of pastoral speech by means of multiple examples drawn from life.[6] For example, a pastor must be capable of addressing the

---

6. Gregory's list of examples and commentary on each is provided on pp. 90-225 of *Pastoral Care*.

poor and rich, the joyful and sad, the wise and dull, the kind and envious, the healthy and sick, the humble and proud, the married and single. "These are the things that a director of souls should observe in the various phases of preaching, so that he may carefully propose the remedies indicated by the wound in each given case. . . . The address must be formulated with such skill that, notwithstanding the diversity of failings in the audience as a whole, it carries a proper message to each individual, without involving itself in contradictions" (PC, 226-27).

The pastor must be watchful, discerning, and sympathetic, displaying a "knowing how" that is analogous to a physician of the body, prescribing medicine "to meet moral diseases by a varied method." Sin is a disease with many symptoms that must be exposed, rooted out by a practiced use of Christian speech, both flexible and fitting, that is capable of converting listeners through the persuasive power of God's curative, healing Word dispensed through Scripture, the instrument of salvation.

For Gregory, preaching is pastoral theology; it is the language "of" faith rather than "about" faith, the articulation of lived wisdom in which doctrine and life are one. Such pastoral discourse was called *psychagogy* in the ancient church, a form of spiritual direction or care, the cure of souls, moral instruction and exhortation that was spoken in a homiletic, or intimate, familiar style.[7] For Gregory, the Son is the Word, but the Holy Spirit is the tongue by which he speaks the word into our minds. Through Christian speech, or sacred rhetoric, the divine doctrine of Scripture seeks to enkindle passionate love for divine wisdom and to evoke moral transformation: a renewed capacity to desire what God desires, the art of living Christ in community.[8]

Gregory and the Bible

Following in the interpretive tradition of Jerome, Ambrose, Origen, and Augustine, Gregory viewed exegesis and the exposition of Scripture as the primary medium of preaching, "a form of pastoral theology exercised in a manner that was practical and profound, and with language both

7. Pierre Hadot, *Philosophy as a Way of Life,* ed. and with an introduction by Arnold I. Davidson, trnas. Michael Chase (Oxford: Blackwell, 1995), pp. 47-78.

8. Jean Leclercq, "From St. Gregory to St. Bernard: From the Sixth to the Twelfth Century," in *A History of Christian Spirituality,* vol. 2: *The Spirituality of the Middle Ages,* pp. 18-19; McGinn, *The Presence of God,* vol. 2, p. 75.

imaginative and persuasive."[9] Scripture was the essential source for all Christian instruction, since it is concerned with one subject: the revelation of God in Christ, the means and goal of salvation. Gregory's whole aim, then, was to point out the way to return to God. Thus, the Bible mirrored the life of Gregory and his listeners in its use: it reflected those vices that should be put off and the virtues that should be put on by the grace of God and human striving toward Christian perfection. To read Scripture, to think and speak about God and the things of God, was, like grammar, not an end in itself. Rather, it was ordered to the love of God as a form of knowledge; its aim was the holiness of the church.[10]

Because Gregory's exegetical work presupposed the historical continuity of the church's tradition of interpretation, faith, and practice, he read Scripture as a unified whole centered in Jesus Christ, the mystery of the Triune God known through Christian worship and sacramental life. The language of the Bible was the servant of theology, knowledge of self and love of God. This characteristic becomes evident in Gregory's most mature work of exegesis, the *Moralia in Job*, a huge work of thirty-five parts that covers the book in its entirety. Robert Wilken notes, "It is a masterful undertaking, a wise, humane book, at once a compendium of the church's teaching on God, Christ, the church, human beings and grace and a matchless guide to the spiritual life."[11]

Gregory delivered the homilies on the Book of Job to monks and clergy in daily monastic collations, or at conferences during his assignment to Constantinople in the 580s. Gregory's exegesis strives for a balance between an inward, allegorical reading to edify faith and a historical interpretation to guide action.[12] The Preface to the *Moralia* provides a

9. Evans, *The Thought of Gregory the Great*, pp. 87-96, here p. 87; see also Henri de Lubac, *Medieval Exegesis: The Four Senses of Scripture*, vol. 1, trans. Mark Sebanc (Grand Rapids: Eerdmans, 1998), pp. 15-74.

10. Robert Wilken, "Interpreting Job Allegorically: The Moralia of Gregory the Great," *Pro Ecclesia* 10, no. 2 (2001): 219-26; Beryl Smalley, *The Study of the Bible in the Middle Ages* (Notre Dame: University of Notre Dame Press, 1964), pp. 32-35; Jean Leclercq, O.S.B., "The Exposition and Exegesis of Scripture," in *The Cambridge History of the Bible*, vol. 2: *The West from the Fathers to the Reformation*, ed. G. W. H. Lampe (Cambridge: Cambridge University Press, 1969), pp. 183-85; McGinn, *The Presence of God*, vol. 2, pp. 39-42.

11. Robert Wilken, *The Spirit of Early Christian Thought: Seeking the Face of God* (New Haven: Yale University Press, 2003), pp. 313-14.

12. Gregory the Great, *Morals on the Book of Job*, 3 vols. (Oxford: Parker, 1844-50); hereafter cited parenthetically in the text as *Morals*.

window through which we may better understand Gregory's practice. Following a brief autobiographical sketch, he revealed his desire to set forth the book of blessed Job, to lay open the mysteries so far as inspiration would be given by the Truth. His task, he said, would be to unveil the words of the history in allegorical senses and to offer a turn of moral exercise that would lead to testimonies — that is, other related places in the Bible. In other words, Gregory's goal was to provide a balanced exposition in the broad expanses of both contemplation and moral instruction to build up the Christian character of his listeners. He described this plan metaphorically through the image of flowing waters:

> For he that treats of sacred writ should follow the way of a river, for if a river, as it flows along its channels, meets with open valleys on its side, into these it immediately turns the course of its current, and when they are copiously supplied, presently it pours itself back into its bed. Thus unquestionably, thus should it be with everyone that treats of the Divine Word, that if, in discussing any subject, he chance to find at hand any occasion of seasonable edification, he should, as it were, force the streams of discourse towards the adjacent valley, and, when he has poured forth enough upon its level of instruction, fall back into the channel of discourse which he had proposed himself. (*Morals*, 6-7)

Gregory's intention was to begin by first laying the historical foundations, the story line; and then, pursuing the typical sense, to "erect a fabric of the mind to be a stronghold of faith"; and finally, to elaborate the grace of moral instruction by "clothing the edifice with coloring." He acknowledged that although the words of Scripture possess a mysterious nature, the Word of God is able to instruct the wise as well as nurse the simpleminded:

> It is, as it were, a kind of river, if I may so liken it, which [is] both shallow and deep, wherein both the lamb may find a footing, and the elephant float at large. Therefore as the fitness of each passage requires, the line of interpretation is studiously varied accordingly, in that the true sense of the word of God is found out with so much the greater fidelity, in proportion as it shifts its course through the different kinds of examples as each case requires. (*Morals*, 8-9)

Rather than pursuing the history behind the text, Gregory's primary concern was to reach out beyond the words to the *res*, the thing itself:

spiritual truth — to seek the face of God revealed by Divine Providence in Sacred History. He declared, "At any rate the Holy Spirit is confidently believed to have been the Author. He then Himself wrote them . . . the Inspirer in the Saint's work" (*Morals*, 14-15). As Robert Wilken comments, "Biblical words are not simply signs that point, they are precious vessels laden with the biblical narrative of the triune God's dealings with human beings. Allegory privileges the language and imagery of the Bible, assuming it is better to use the words of the Bible to speak matters of faith and life than to translate them into an alien idiom."[13] The Old Testament, therefore, is read as the church's book, Christian Scripture.

Gregory's accommodation of exegesis for the edification of his clerical and monastic listeners appears in the latter parts of the exposition. In Part Five, after briefly reprising Job's story, Gregory announces that Christ, the Only Begotten, shines forth in all the words and events of Job's life (*Morals*, 5.24.1-55). Christ is the Light of allegory himself, one with his Holy Church who, in his passion and sufferings, is the Mediator who bears the travails of the church. In similar manner, Job's friends are the type of heretics who speak with the folly of pride; speaking right things but in the wrong way, they are corrupted with arrogance. On the other hand, Job is a type of the church to whom the heretics must return in a spirit of humility. Pointing to the mystery of Christ, the narrative of Job provided the means by which Gregory encouraged listeners to depend upon the miracle of the Word, which by grace grants the virtue of renewal (*Morals*, 3.24.1-53).

Building on the foundation of "Our Lord Jesus Christ, in that He is the Power and Wisdom of God," Gregory proceeded to interpret the images in Job 38 — light, heat, showers, and thunder — as signifying the providential opening that God makes for his Word, the "voice of grace." He declared that the Spirit, a gift from on high, irradiates the mind, tempers the heat of temptation and persecution, and works within the hearts of listeners to strengthen fearless preachers whose words press from without. The words of holy preachers, furthermore, are like refreshing showers that quench the thirsty hearts of God's elect; however, without the assistance of divine grace, the Lord's internal witness, they cannot pass like arrows into the hearts of hearers. The trials and tortures of the present world notwithstanding, the proclamation of belief in eternal joy

13. Wilken, "Interpreting Job Allegorically," pp. 221-22.

45

is like a "violent" shower, which, when authorized by God, speaks through the boundless power of preaching.

In like manner, the Incarnate Lord thunders with terror, speaking through the words of the Prophets and the Apostles to open deaf ears and pierce hardened hearts. In God's mercy the rain of preaching showers dry, barren desert — the church — producing fresh herbs, the fruit of good works: inward inspiration added to outward words causes parched hearts to become green, the closed to be opened, the empty to be filled, the hungry to be fed, and the unfruitful to germinate. The Word of God, spoken and heard with the power of divine charity, is returned with an abundance of increase (*Morals*, 302, 333-39).

The *Moralia in Job* represents the most frequent expression of Gregory's preaching: sermons delivered to various degrees of ecclesiastical leadership. His undertaking of this task was similar to that of Augustine, who, in *De Doctrina Christiana,* conversed with pastors on how Scripture is to be expounded for the church. On the other hand, the most important record of Gregory's popular, liturgical preaching is contained in the *Homilies on the Gospels,* which were delivered either by Gregory or, in his absence due to illness, by others at various sites in Rome during the early 590s, when political and economic conditions turned increasingly difficult. Because these homilies were preached to the general public, Gregory's scriptural exposition is brief, direct, and without allegory. He prefers to dwell on the literal or moral sense for large, diverse audiences, choosing to focus on Christ and the shape of Christian life devoted to him.[14]

The *Homily on Luke 2:1-14,* which presumably was written to be preached at Christmas, offers an excellent example of Gregory's popular preaching. In the introduction he refers to the festal occasion of the Nativity, stating that because he must celebrate the Eucharist three times during the day, his comments on the Gospel lesson will be brief. The content of the homily stays close to the text of Scripture; its attention is directed to Christ and to how the circumstances of his birth disclose the redemptive ministry of his Incarnation. Just as the world was enrolled in the imperial census, so he came to enroll the elect in eternity. Similarly, just as he was born in Bethlehem, the "house of bread," so he in his body

---

14. Markus, *Gregory the Great and His World,* pp. 35-50; Gregory the Great, *Forty Gospel Homilies,* trans. Dom David Hurst (Kalamazoo, Mich.: Cistercian Publications, 1990).

is Bread from Heaven. And just as he was born not at home but on the road, so he in his coming to a truly foreign place did still remain eternal.[15]

The site of Christ's birth also serves to interpret his saving work. Just as he changed the hay of humanity to wheat by lying in a manger, so he nourishes believers who aspire to holiness with the hay of his body, heavenly food. Just as the angels appeared to the shepherds and the brightness of God shone around them, so pastors, shepherds of Christ's flock, are privileged to see lofty things by the gift of divine grace, which shines upon them. The heart of the homily, however, is a brief summary of the person and work of Christ, God in human form. Following the example of the angels, Gregory announced that Christ was born as King; thus all who honor and acknowledge him are made citizens of the kingdom of heaven. Even the angels worshiped Christ; because he took upon himself bodily weakness, sinful humanity is no longer despised. Gregory concludes with an exhortation to his listeners to live as God's citizens, to preserve the high dignity given in Christ by taking up a holy way of life: "because God became a human being, human beings have been called gods."[16]

Gregory's pastoral use of Scripture was fused with the theological practice of prayerful, loving attention to God. Bernard McGinn observes, "The main lines of his understanding of the nature of contemplation can only be understood by seeing how the pope viewed the history of salvation as essentially a history of contemplation . . . the Christian story of creation, fall, and redemption."[17] Gregory thus viewed himself and his people as actors in that story rather than detached observers; both clergy and laity were called to participate in a transformation of life through ascetic habits of prayer, repentance, and self-denial expressed in works of charity. The goal of pastoral exegesis or theology in preaching is both personal and corporate conversion. The object of understanding Scripture's "sacred eloquence" is that the church be renewed by the power to live as it speaks.[18]

---

15. Gregory the Great, *Homily on Luke 2:1-14*, in *Forty Gospel Homilies*, pp. 50-51.

16. Gregory the Great, *Homily on Luke 2:1-14*, in *Forty Gospel Homilies*, pp. 52-53.

17. McGinn, "Contemplation in Gregory the Great," in *Gregory the Great: A Symposium*, ed. John C. Cavadini (Notre Dame: University of Notre Dame Press, 1995), p. 146.

18. Markus, *Gregory the Great and His World*, pp. 43-45; Conrad Leyser, *Authority and Asceticism from Augustine to Gregory the Great* (Oxford: Clarendon Press, 2000), pp. 162-75.

Saint Benedict: Monastic Exemplar

From the initial triumph of monasticism in the fourth century through its flowering in the twelfth, it was inevitable that theology should become monastic. During this time the majority of significant theological figures were monks, inhabiting a particular spiritual environment, speaking to and writing for monks, commenting on Scripture to instruct and shape the experience of monks. During the fifth and sixth centuries, moreover, a desire for the contemplative life grew in amazing proportions into a protest movement throughout both East and West. In the West, monasticism, which was carried westward through several channels, started late but became immediately popular in an age of extreme cultural disruption, ascetical renunciation, and, most important, increasing desire for God.[19]

By the sixth century, monasteries were scattered all over Europe, mission outposts committed to the task of evangelization and re-evangelization. Yet, in comparison with all other forms or rules of monastic life, the Rule of St. Benedict stands out as a masterpiece of evangelical faith and human wisdom.

Benedict and the Rule

What we know of Benedict comes from what Gregory the Great said of him in the second book of his *Dialogues,* a work of monastic hagiography. Gregory's narrative presents Benedict as the "man of God," an ascetic monk, and above all, the abbot, a Christian who renounced the world and overcame temptation, attained self-control in union with God, became capable of exercising spiritual fatherhood, and received, for the good of those around him, gifts similar to those of the saints of the Old and New Testaments.[20]

19. C. H. Lawrence, *Medieval Monasticism* (New York: Longman, 1984), pp. 1-35; Lawrence, *Western Society and the Church in the Middle Ages* (New York: Penguin Books, 1990), pp. 214-30; Louis Bouyer, "Primitive and Patristic Period: Love and Knowledge of God," in *A History of Christian Spirituality,* vol. 1: *The Spirituality of the New Testament and the Fathers* (New York: Seabury Press, 1982), pp. 455-529; McGinn, *The Presence of God,* vol. 2, pp. 24-34.

20. Lawrence, *Medieval Monasticism,* pp. 18-23; Jean Leclercq, O.S.B., *The Love of Learning and the Desire for God: A Study of Monastic Culture,* trans. Catherine Misrahi (New York: Fordham University Press, 1982), pp. 11-36; Bouyer, "Latin Monasticism from St. Augustine to St. Gregory," in *The Spirituality of the New Testament and the Fathers,* pp. 512-19.

Of significance for the monastic tradition in Gregory's brief treatment is Benedict's conversion, which was similar to St. Augustine's, and his devotion to studies, a love of learning joined to a means of searching for God: the love of eternal life. Interestingly, in the *Dialogues* Gregory makes only a single reference to St. Benedict's Rule, but in so doing he unites the saint's words with his life:

"He wrote a Rule for monks remarkable for its discretion and the lucidity of its language. If anyone wishes to know more about his life and conversation, he can find all the facts of the master's teaching in this same institution of the Rule, for the holy man could not teach otherwise than he lived."[21]

The prologue and first several chapters of the Rule comprise an exhortatory treatise on the ascetical life, explaining its aims and the characteristic virtues the monk (*monos*, meaning "alone," "single," or "one with God") should strive to cultivate, foremost among which are obedience and humility. The following thirteen chapters contain detailed instructions for the order of divine service — the regular round of prayer, readings, and psalmody, which constitutes the framework of the monk's day. Following this are a series of chapters dealing with constitutional matters such as the election of the abbot and the role of the other monastic officers, regulations for meals, and a penitential code, which lays down penalties for breaches of the monastic discipline. In addition, much attention is devoted to the reception and training of recruits. C. H. Lawrence comments, "As a whole, the Rule offered an eminently practical guide both to the government of a cenobitical community and [to] the spiritual life of the monk."[22]

According to Benedict, the monastic life has no other purpose than to provide a stable environment for the search for God and union with God, which entails making the First Commandment the whole of one's life, integrating moral virtue, spiritual contemplation, and asceticism. Life in the monastery aims to be entirely disinterested, a "school for the service of the Lord" rather than any other practical or social end; monks are simply seeking to be formed to perfection as citizens in the kingdom of Christ.

21. Cited in Lawrence, *Medieval Monasticism*, p. 19.
22. Lawrence, *Medieval Monasticism*, p. 21. Here I am following *The Rule of Saint Benedict*, translated and with an introduction and notes by Anthony C. Meisel and M. L. del Mastro (New York: Doubleday-Image, 1975); hereafter cited parenthetically in the text as *RSB*.

Moreover, only obedience, "to listen, or to hear God" in rapt attention, attentive regard for the Word will form the monk to the basic virtue, which now appears as humility. Significantly, Benedict's whole doctrine of spiritual progress, the search for God, consists in his teaching on the degrees of humility, openness to grace, or receptivity to the love of Christ revealed through one's abbot, Scripture, the liturgy, and communal life. As the perfect disposability to the divine will manifested in all things, humility becomes the source of perfection itself, of the flowering of true charity (RSB, Prologue):

> When the monk has climbed all twelve steps, he will find the perfect love of God, which casts out all fear, by means of which everything he had observed anxiously before will now appear simple and natural. He will no longer act out of the fear of Hell, but for the love of Christ, out of good habits and with a pleasure derived of virtue. The Lord, through the Holy Spirit, will show this to His servant, cleansed of sin and vice. (RSB, 61)[23]

Benedict thus placed stability, obedience, and humility in the service of God to construct a vision of the life of faith constituted by communal worship and prayer, private reading, devotion, and physical labor rooted in and manifesting the life of the Gospel as taught and embodied by Christ. Moreover, monastic life was lived with particular intensity, since it was a school, *scola*, for the Lord's service, a term with a military as well as an academic sense. The monastery was thus viewed as a kind of spiritual combat unit, engaged in a struggle to maintain loving awareness of God in a world in which the contemplation of divine things had become increasingly obscured by worldly pursuits and excessive self-love.[24]

A central characteristic of St. Benedict's Rule is its focus on the initiative and sovereign action of divine grace, the agency of Christ in the Spirit, who evokes the praise and glorification of God. This is the basic activity and attitude, present in every aspect of a monk's work, prayer, and study — *lectio divina*, which seeks the experience of divine love and longs for its completion in communion. To this end, specific periods of study were designated, structuring days, weeks, months, and seasons, setting forth the frequency of and conditions for silent reading and, more

23. Bouyer, "Latin Monasticism from St. Augustine to St. Gregory," pp. 514-17.
24. Lawrence, *Medieval Monasticism*, pp. 23-28.

important, for reading aloud, a "chewing and tasting" of Scripture allowing monks to hear the "voice of the page." Monastic reading was a journey that enabled spiritual pilgrims to advance from page to page, a practice requiring readers' full engagement with all the senses of mind and
body (*RSB*, 61-69).[25]

In commending "divine reading," Benedict perceived that the work
of God, the *opus Dei*, eight periods of formal, oral, and communal prayer
spaced throughout the day and night, would unite monks in voicing creation's praise for its Maker to become a living doxology — "with our
minds in harmony with our voices" — drawing them into ever deepening participation in the life of God. Thus the value of the work of God,
the *opus Dei*, lies not so much in the fact that it is a work or a service
(*opus*) but in the fact that it is the service *of God*. Everything the monks do
is in the service of God, which fills their minds with God's truth in order
to unite them with God's love in a union of wills.[26] As Stanley Hauerwas
comments, "The monks have been right to think nothing is more important for the shaping of communities of holiness than how our days are
structured. Nothing is more important for holiness than learning to
speak and the use of that speech to speak the truth to one another in
love."[27]

Yet, even for Benedict himself, all that he wrote was insufficient to
make a perfect Christian, unless to this observance there should be added
the seventy-third and final chapter of the Rule to inspire participants in
the monastic life to go on to its completion:

> We have composed this Rule so that, through its observance in monas-
> teries, we may know we have made some progress in pursuit of virtue
> and the commitment of a monastic life. For those who are hurrying to
> attain a truly holy life, there are the works of the Fathers. The following

---

25. See the excellent discussion of *lectio divina* in Leclercq, *The Love of Learning and the
Desire for God*, pp. 15-20, 72-73; Ivan Illich, *In the Vineyard of the Text: A Commentary to Hugh's
"Didascalicon"* (Chicago: University of Chicago Press, 1993), pp. 43-45, 107-10; Paul Griffiths,
Religious Reading: The Place of Reading in the Practice of Religion (New York: Oxford University
Press, 1999), p. ix; Michael Casey, *Sacred Reading: The Ancient Art of Lectio Divina* (Liguori:
Liguori/Triumph, 1996).

26. Thomas Merton, *Bread in the Wilderness* (New York: New Direction Books, 1997),
pp. 12-14.

27. Hauerwas, *Sanctify Them in the Truth: Holiness Exemplified* (Nashville: Abingdon Press,
1998), p. 90.

of these will lead a man to the heights of perfection. For what page or word of the Bible is not a perfect rule for temporal life? What book of the Fathers does not proclaim that by a straight path we shall find God? What else but examples of virtue of good living, obedient monks are the Collations, Institutes, Lives of the Saints, of the Holy Fathers, and the Rule of St. Basil? We who are slothful, bad living and careless should be afraid. Whoever you are, if you wish to follow the path to God, make use of this little Rule for beginners. Thus at length you will come to the heights of doctrine and virtue under God's guidance. Amen! (RSB, 106)

The Rule on Monasticism and Scripture

The Prologue of the Rule of St. Benedict urged monastic communities to awaken from spiritual slumber by attending to the Word of God:

> Let us rise without delay, the Scriptures stirring us. . . . Let us open our eyes to the Divine light and attentively hear the Divine voice calling and exhorting us daily: "Today if you shall hear his voice, harden not your hearts" (Ps. 95:7-8), and again, "He who has ears, let him hear what the Spirit says to the Churches" (Rev. 2:7). (RSB, Prologue)

What was sought in Scripture, "the school of the Lord's service," was to acquire only one skill — to learn Christ, since it is in Scripture that the Christian finds the deepest mysteries of God revealed and there begins the contemplation of ultimate truth and the love of ultimate good:[28]

> As our loves and paths progress, the heart expands and with the sweetness of love we move down the paths of God's commandments. Never departing from his guidance, remaining in the monastery until death, we patiently share in Christ's passion so we may eventually enter into the Kingdom of God. (RSB, 45)

Monks habitually read Scripture in consultation with the Fathers; theology, *theologia*, was interchangeable with *sacra scriptura*, or *sacra pagina*. The *ethos* for scriptural reading was the divine economy, the manifestation of God's love for humanity, and the Christian life, seen as human ap-

---

28. Merton, *Bread in the Wilderness*, pp. 133-38.

propriation of this same love. "Scripture was a *speculum* (mirror) in which to see the self, either as it is in actuality or as it might be someday."[29]

The cultivation of so deep a "biblical imagination" through careful, detailed study of Scripture was achieved through living participation in the creedal and catechetical tradition of the Catholic Church, in the spiritual atmosphere and celebration of its liturgy and prayer. Monastic reading, then, *lectio divina*, was not so much for the text itself, to solve intellectual and moral problems, but for reading and gaining personal benefit. The aim was to taste, to savor the Word of God, that the contemplative life of prayer and union might be strengthened; Scripture was a means of leading souls to God. Jean Leclercq comments, "Christ, the Word of God, was the heart of the liturgy and the Bible. . . . In thanksgiving [the soul] offers to the Father that divine sonship, which it receives from the Word, the spouse of the soul, with the gift of the Spirit of the Father and the Son."[30]

Moreover, monastic reading approached the Bible as a unified whole in Christ, since it is concerned with the whole mystery of salvation: what God is, what God does for humanity, from the beginning to the end of the world. At the center of the narrative of creation and sanctification is the Son of God made flesh, the Incarnation; all that preceded Christ's coming, all that accompanied it, and all that follows must be understood in relation to him. The principle underlying monastic exegesis is that the mystery of Christ and the church is a growing body sustained across time, the *totus Christus*, the "total Christ."

Thus the history of the chosen people is instructive in the present, just as the spiritual interpretation of the Old Testament is the beginning of what will one day be vision; salvation history still has a future. Such reading kindles eschatological desire and nourishes not only faith but hope and love as well. As Leclercq further explains, "Spiritual exegesis is that in which the hidden mystery is apprehended and applied to the life of the soul and all that concerns it: asceticism, mysticism, the Church, the sacraments, and eschatology. But in all these there is realized the sole object of the Scriptures, union with Christ."[31]

29. Peter S. Hawkins, *Dante's Testaments: Essays in Scriptural Imagination* (Palo Alto, Calif.: Stanford University Press, 1999), p. 23. See also Jean Leclercq, O.S.B., "From Gregory to St. Bernard," in *The Cambridge History of the Bible*, vol. 2: *The West from the Fathers to the Reformation*, pp. 183-96.

30. Leclercq, "From Gregory to St. Bernard," pp. 191-92.

31. Leclercq, "From Gregory to St. Bernard," p. 196; Leclercq, *The Love of Learning and the*

Bernard of Clairvaux: "Doctor Mellifluus"

The eleventh and twelfth centuries, especially the years between 1040 and 1160, were a period of intense, rapid, and to a high degree self-conscious change in almost all aspects of human thought and activity, including an intense concern with the nature of religious life and the personal reform of all Christians. Traditional institutions and attitudes were stretched to the maximum and made to accommodate new forms of life and new sentiments. In France, Cîteaux, and the order that sprang from it, the Cistercians, came out of the same restless search for a simpler and more secluded form of ascetical life that found expression in other new orders in the eleventh century. Like similar movements, it began as a reaction against the corporate wealth, worldly involvements, and stale liturgical ritualism of the older monastic tradition.[32]

The founders of Cîteaux aimed at restoring the pristine observance of the Benedictine Rule. The "new monastery" became the archetype of a new order dedicated to a revival by getting back to the spirit of literal observance of the Rule of St. Benedict. According to Bernard McGinn, "The goal of the New Monastery was to create a 'school of love' which would enable the new humanity inaugurated by Christ to flourish, a humanity empowered by the Holy Spirit alive in the soul and manifesting his presence through humility and charity."[33]

During the second quarter of the twelfth century, the influence of Bernard of Clairvaux, "the last of the Fathers" (d. 1153), was unsurpassed among monastic leaders and advocates of reform. Bernard almost single-handedly assured the survival and success of the order of Cîteaux through his personal moral force and powers of persuasion, owing to his gifts and stature as abbot, writer, mystical theologian, counselor to popes and monarchs, and preacher.[34]

Desire for God, pp. 71-88; Aidan Nichols, O.P., *The Shape of Catholic Theology: An Introduction to Its Sources, Principles, and History* (Collegeville, Minn.: Liturgical Press, 1991), pp. 288-90.

32. Lawrence, *Medieval Monasticism*, pp. 146-55; Lawrence, *Western Society and the Church in the Middle Ages*, pp. 250-71; John A. F. Thomson, *The Western Church in the Middle Ages* (London: Arnold; New York: Oxford University Press, 1998), pp. 111-17; Giles Constable, *The Reformation of the Twelfth Century* (Cambridge: Cambridge University Press, 1996), pp. 1-43.

33. McGinn, *The Presence of God*, vol. 2, p. 162. See also the general discussion, pp. 149-57.

34. For introductions to Bernard's life and work, I have followed these texts: McGinn, *The Presence of God*, vol. 2, pp. 158-224; Leclercq, "The School of Citeaux," in *A History of*

Bernard was honored with the title *Doctor Mellifluus*, which means "the Doctor whose teaching is as sweet as honey" or, more literally, "the Doctor flowing with honey." The title is significant, since it refers to a kind of sweetness that overflows from the goodness, mercy, and charity of God attained in contemplating the hidden mysteries of Christ in sacred Scripture. Bernard's theology, however, was traditional: his mystical experience and the preaching that was a primary means of its expression were firmly grounded in the Church's Trinitarian faith and established practices.[35]

Strengthening the Christian Life

Bernard's primary purpose was indeed practical: to build up and strengthen others, allowing traditional monastic wisdom derived from Scripture and the Fathers to assist those seeking to live an evangelical life and make progress toward God in loving prayer. Moreover, Bernard's vision of the human journey to God spanned all the stages of salvation history: we are formed in the image of God, deformed by sin, and reformed by the grace of being conformed to Christ; we look forward to being transformed in glory at the end of time.[36] According to Bernard, we are made to love God, which requires freedom, the work of grace, for living out our baptismal vocation by following the Gospel of Christ. Bernard's

---

Christian Spirituality, vol. 2: *The Spirituality of the Middle Ages,* pp. 187-218; Leclercq, "Introduction," in *Bernard of Clairvaux: Selected Works,* translated and with a foreword by G. R. Evans (Mahwah, N.J.: Paulist Press, 1987), pp. 13-57; Étienne Gilson, *The Mystical Theology of Saint Bernard,* trans. A. H. C. Downes (London and New York: Sheed & Ward, 1955); G. R. Evans, *Bernard of Clairvaux* (New York: Oxford University Press, 2000); Evans, *The Mind of St. Bernard of Clairvaux* (Oxford: Clarendon Press, 1983).

35. Jaroslav Pelikan observes, "In the West, orthodoxy and asceticism have been mutually supportive. A particularly brilliant example is the career of Bernard of Clairvaux in the twelfth century." See his *Credo: Historical and Theological Guide to "Creeds and Confessions of Faith in the Christian Tradition"* (New Haven and London: Yale University Press, 2003), p. 297. See also Thomas Merton, *The Last of the Fathers: Saint Bernard of Clairvaux and the Encyclical Letter, Doctor Mellifluus* (New York: Harcourt, Brace & Company, 1954), pp. 9-15; Henri de Lubac, S.J., *Medieval Exegesis: The Four Senses of Scripture,* vol. 2, trans. E. M. Macierowski (Grand Rapids: Eerdmans, 2000), pp. 162-70.

36. Michael Casey, O.C.S.O., "Bernard of Clairvaux, St., 1090-1153: French Cistercian Reformer and Theologian," in *Encyclopedia of Monasticism,* ed. William M. Johnston, vol. 1, A-L (Chicago and London: Fitzroy Dearborn Publishers, 2000), pp. 144-46.

doctrine, then, is wisdom, which rises to a knowledge of God and of the things of God in the infinite riches of the love of Christ. The Bible therefore tells a love story of God and his people, God and his church, God and each person that leads humanity back to God, which determines how it is to be read and preached.[37]

This conviction was affirmed by two of Bernard's best-known treatises: *On the Steps of Humility and Pride* and *On Loving God*. In the light of the self-knowledge acquired in deepening humility through loving attention to the humanity of Christ, the gift of charity displaces fear: one comes to love oneself only in God, proceeding from the "region of unlikeness" to the likeness of God, from carnal to spiritual love. Moreover, because God is the goal of life and God is love, proper human desire seeks to achieve union with God, conforming one's will to the divine will. Human happiness, the whole work of salvation, consists in nothing else but the restoration of this order of charity, the will and ability for which come from the Incarnate Word, the source of all our strength. In addition, Christ's role in the reformation of the image and likeness is rooted in the function of the Word in creation and in consummation. Humility is the fitting point of departure, while the destination is a spiritual perception. Love of God is experienced as joy, delight, sweetness, and savor; contemplation is communicated in fruitful service to the church.[38]

Preaching the Love of God

Sermons were arguably Bernard's most significant form of service or ministry to the church; he preferred to cast his most important theological productions in the sermonic genre. In addition, he was the most prominent preacher during a revival of preaching, both in monasteries and in the church abroad. Robert of Basevorn, writing in the fourteenth century, a period when the genre, the *ars predicandi* (art of preaching), flourished, lists Bernard as one of the church's five great preachers, along with Christ, Paul, Augustine, and Gregory. He describes Bernard's homiletic method and its enduring value:

37. Leclercq, "Introduction," in *Bernard of Clairvaux: Selected Works*, pp. 30-35.

38. Gilson, *The Mystical Theology of Saint Bernard*, pp. 119-54; McGinn, *The Presence of God*, vol. 2, pp. 166-78; Ellen T. Charry, *By the Renewing of Your Minds: The Pastoral Function of Christian Doctrine* (New York: Oxford University Press, 1997), pp. 177-78; Leclercq, "The School of Citeaux," pp. 194-96.

The method of Saint Bernard is without method, exceeding the style of capability of all men of genius. He more than all the rest stresses Scripture in all his sayings so that scarcely one statement is his own which does not depend upon an authority in the bible or a multitude of authorities. His procedure is always devout, always artful. He takes a certain theme or something in place of it and begins it artfully, divides it into two, three, or many members, confirms it and ends it, using every rhetorical color so that the whole work shines with a double glow, earthly and heavenly; this . . . invites to devotion those who understand more feelingly, and helps more in the novel methods which we are now discussing. No one has so effectively joined the two at the same time.[39]

Robert's description touches on important characteristics of Bernard's preaching as a monk: deep immersion in Scripture, loving devotion to God, reliance upon patristic and classical traditions, artful speech that is luminous with spiritual wisdom for the fulfillment of the Christian life.

Bernard modeled his thinking and speaking on Scripture, which expresses the divine mystery in human words; the formation of Christian speech is the cumulative effect of *lectio divina,* of opening the mind and heart to hear the divine voice in and through the language of sacred Scripture. "Speaking Scripture," then, is a mode of exegesis embodied in the whole of life, the fruit of virtuous living in obedience to the commandments of God and out of love for God; "it is a way of being and a style of life, experienced wisdom according to reason, the true or heavenly philosophy."[40]

For Bernard, preaching is simply communicating to others, by means of poetic speech, what he knows through experience — the love of God. Speaking of God is an expression of the primary aims of monastic life — "the love of learning and the desire for God" — while the bestowal of divine grace lends rhetorical beauty and grandeur to this discourse. Moreover, eloquence is an instrument but never an end, while elegant style is homage paid to God that belongs to the Spirit, whose nature is to communicate himself. Preaching is not merely informative but also trans-

39. Cited in James J. Murphy, *Rhetoric in the Middle Ages: A History of Rhetorical Theory from Saint Augustine to the Renaissance* (Berkeley and Los Angeles: University of California Press, 1974), p. 347.
40. Hadot, *Philosophy as a Way of Life,* p. 133.

formative for those who speak and listen, "an invitation to join a conversation between lovers."[41]

Bernard's greatest masterpiece was a series of sermons, eighty-six in all, on the Song of Songs, the Canticle of Canticles, which he began in 1135 and continued until his death in 1153. Bernard considered the Canticle to be a contemplative text, a *theoricus sermo*. Leclercq observes, "With its ardent language and its dialogue of praise, it was more attuned than any other book in Sacred Scripture to loving, disinterested contemplation."[42]

Bernard set out his key ideas and direction at the beginning of the sermons. The Song of Songs is a poem in praise of Christ and his church, sung to the King of Kings and Lord of Lords, expressing the deepest longings of the sanctified soul. Thus, in hearing its words, monks should hunger not for milk but rather for fine, flavorsome bread; it will be necessary to break open the book to nourish receptive hearts (*BC*, 210). Proverbs and Ecclesiastes, the first of Solomon's books, set forth morals and wisdom to heal the evils of excessive self-love and empty love of the world, returning readers to the fear of God and obedience to his commandments. The Canticle, on the other hand, is holy contemplative discourse; it is the fruit of the first two books, which feeds seriously inclined ears and minds with the wisdom of the Spirit (*BC*, 211).

Bernard humbly implores his listeners to look not to him but rather to God for such wisdom, since he too must beg for food to nourish soul

41. Leclercq, *The Love of Learning and the Desire for God*, pp. 167-76, 260-68, here p. 169; also Evans, *The Mind of St. Bernard of Clairvaux*, pp. 72-108; Evans, *Bernard of Clairvaux*, pp. 57-66. See also the discussion of monastic preaching as a liturgical act in Chrysogonus Waddell, "The Liturgical Dimension of Twelfth-Century Cistercian Preaching," in *Medieval Monastic Preaching*, ed. Carolyn Muessig (Leiden: Brill, 1998), pp. 335-50. A good introduction to Bernard's preaching is provided in *Bernard of Clairvaux: Sermons for the Summer Season: Liturgical Sermons from Rogationtide and Pentecost*, trans. Beverly Mayne Kienzle (Kalamazoo, Mich.: Cistercian Publications, 1991), pp. 3-26.

42. I am using the sermons in Evans, *Bernard of Clairvaux: Selected Works*, 207-78; hereafter cited parenthetically in the text as *BC*. See the discussion in Leclercq, *The Love of Learning and the Desire for God*, pp. 84-86; Leclercq, "Introduction," in *Bernard of Clairvaux: Selected Works*, pp. 45-57; McGinn, *The Presence of God*, vol. 2, pp. 164-65; Michael Casey, *A Thirst for God: Spiritual Desire in Bernard of Clairvaux's Sermons on the Song of Songs* (Kalamazoo, Mich.: Cistercian Publications, 1988). Whether Bernard's written sermons represent what was actually preached is a matter of historical debate. See Christopher Holdsworth, "Were the Sermons of St. Bernard on the Song of Songs Ever Preached?" in *Medieval Monastic Preaching*, ed. Muessig, pp. 295-318.

and spirit, just as he too must ask, seek, and knock: "O most Kind, break your bread for those who are hungering for it by my hands if you allow, but by your power." Bernard then shifts to his next theme: "Tell us, by whom, about whom, and to whom it is said, 'Let him kiss me with the kiss of his mouth'?" This delightful metaphor is a beginning kiss; the loving face of Scripture draws readers to search for divine treasure hidden in the sweetness of its discourse. Thus "beginning without a beginning" is a fresh expression of an old book, a sign of the art of the Spirit and a source of delight. It is indeed appropriate to begin the book with a sign of peace, the Kiss, and Solomon, the Peacemaker. More important, those whose minds are at peace are invited to understand the teaching of Scripture, to master disturbances caused by vices and tumults of care (*BC*, 212).

Bernard's allegorical interpretation enlarges upon the Canticle, privileging the biblical language to render its "spiritual sense." Through his interpretation of the Old Testament in light of the cross and resurrection, as a book about Christ and the church, exegesis and mysticism are interwoven and grounded in the patristic doctrine of union with God.[43] Bernard emphasizes that the book's title is not merely "Song" but "Song of Songs," since it embraces the many songs and singers within the whole of Scripture: Deborah, Judith, the mother of Samuel, and the Prophets, who sang to God out of gratitude for a victory, for an edifying example, for others, for escape from danger, for a long-awaited gift. However, Solomon was divinely inspired to sing the praises of Christ and the church out of gratitude for the gift of holy love and the mystery of eternal union with God; this is the wedding song and longing of the holy soul, its exulting in the Spirit (*BC*, 213).

According to Bernard, such figurative language is voiced by one who sang with veiled face in the presence of divine glory, an experience, however, that may now be shared by all who are ready and willing to hear the Song: "Sing to the Lord himself a new song because he has done marvel-

---

43. See the excellent descriptions of allegorical exegesis in de Lubac, *Medieval Exegesis: The Four Senses of Scripture*, vol. 2, pp. 83-125, 153-56; Robert L. Wilken, "Introduction," in *The Song of Songs: Interpreted by Early Christian and Medieval Commentators*, trans. and ed. Richard A. Norris Jr. (Grand Rapids: Eerdmans, 2004); Wilken, "In Defense of Allegory," in *Theology and Scriptural Imagination*, ed. L. Gregory Jones and James J. Buckley (Oxford: Blackwell, 1998), pp. 35-50. See also Sandra M. Schneiders, I.H.M., "Biblical Spirituality," *Interpretation* 56, no. 2 (April 2002): 133-42; Mark S. Burrows, "To Taste with the Heart," *Interpretation* 56, no. 2 (April 2002): 168-80.

ous things!" Bernard's exclamation is an invitation for listeners to hear echoed in the Canticle's poetic narrative their own experience of salvation: repentance, forgiveness of sins, newness of life, promise of eternal rewards, and the joy of bread from heaven. Such doxological living is continually renewed by the offering of thanksgiving for each victory won, each temptation overcome, each vice subdued, each danger avoided, each tempter's trap detected, each passion cured, each virtue received. For Bernard, the Song of Songs is a "Song of steps" taken upward in the heart, a song of praise and glory to God (BC, 214).

Bernard concludes by commending the sweetness of the Song that outshines all others; it is their fruit by the inspiration of the Holy Spirit. It is neither noise made aloud nor sounds on the lips, but rather the music of the heart, a stirring of joy and a harmony of wills. Only he who sings and he to whom it is sung may hear it — the Bridegroom and his bride, Christ and the church, the Word and the soul: "It is a wedding song indeed, expressing the embrace of chaste and joyful souls, the concord of their lives and the mutual exchange of their love" (BC, 215).

CHAPTER 3

Medieval Voices
in the Story of Sacred Rhetoric

In the thirteenth century, the mendicant orders were founded during a time of increasingly passionate desire for spiritual and moral renewal, for new forms of Christian living that aimed toward the purity of the Gospel. This was a time of looking back to Scripture and the Fathers in order to look forward, to address the pressing needs of both church and society, which were in the midst of exciting and challenging intellectual discoveries and rapid social and economic change. The Franciscans and the Dominicans were two of the most significant orders that were founded, respectively, by Francis of Assisi in Italy and Dominic of Guzman in Spain. These two orders, which embodied distinctive rules or ways of life, rose to prominence in large part because of their theological and pastoral work, especially preaching, among Europe's expanding urban populations.

The story of the Preaching Friars provides a wealth of insight for better understanding the kind of intellectual, spiritual, and moral training required to faithfully and effectively communicate the Gospel in changing conditions and diverse circumstances, for challenging and correcting doctrinal heresies, and for evangelizing the faithful. Two of their most important representatives, Bonaventure of the Franciscans and Thomas Aquinas of the Dominicans, are exemplars whose integrative wisdom illumines the vocation of preaching in its fullness.

Bonaventure: Exemplar of the Franciscans

Historical Context

The emergence of the Franciscans and the Dominicans in the early thir-teenth century occurred in a world where the religious monopoly of the medieval church was being challenged by radical heretical groups, and at the same time was facing fresh demands created by the impact of eco-nomic, social, and intellectual changes. The orders of the mendicant fri-ars represented "a new and revolutionary form of the religious life, and was seen by some as a providential response to a spiritual crisis afflicting western Christendom." Put simply, this crisis was a confrontation be-tween traditional assumptions about the nature of the Christian life and the religious needs of a newly arisen urban and secular culture, where it seemed to many that these needs could no longer be met by established forms of religious organization.[1]

This was most true in the cities where a relative freedom from cus-tomary bonds, increasing and shifting populations, political self-consciousness and turbulence, the constant stimulus of competition, and the increase of literacy among the laity stimulated both orthodox criti-cism of the church and radical dissent. Already in the eleventh century, through the reforms initiated by Pope Gregory VII, and in the twelfth century, through a renaissance of learning and piety, there had been at-tempts to revive the monastic call to the desert in order to recreate the model of Christianity embodied in the New Testament. This was called the *vita apostolica* — the apostolic life, which was perceived as necessary for facilitating an engagement between the Gospel and a rapidly changing secular world.[2]

Francis of Assisi (d. 1226), son of Pietro Bernardone, a prosperous clothes merchant who lived in one of twelfth-century Italy's most turbu-lent societies, heard the call of Christ in a dream while on his way to wage

---

1. C. H. Lawrence, *The Friars: The Impact of the Early Mendicant Movement on Western Soci-ety* (New York: Longman, 1994), pp. 1-26; R. W. Southern, *Western Society and the Church in the Middle Ages* (London: Penguin Books, 1990), pp. 270-79; Bernard McGinn, *The Presence of God*, vol. 3: *The Flowering of Mysticism: Men and Women in the New Mysticism* (New York: Cross-road Publishing, 1998), pp. 1-30.

2. John A. T. Thomson, *The Western Church in the Middle Ages* (New York: Oxford Uni-versity Press, 1998), pp. 119-24.

war against a neighboring community. Later, while he was attending mass in the humble oratory at Portiuncula, God spoke to him through the voice of the priest who read the Gospel lesson from Matthew 10:

> Go, said the Saviour, and proclaim everywhere that the kingdom of Heaven is upon you. You received without cost; give without charge. Take no gold, silver, or copper in your belt, no pack for the road, no second coat, no sandals, no stick, for the worker deserves his keep. Whatever town or village you enter, look for some worthy person in it, and stay with him until you leave. And when you go into a house, salute it by saying: Peace on this house.[3]

Renouncing his family patrimony and home, Francis embarked on a spiritual quest that led him to assume a deeply joyful yet ascetical life modeled after the suffering, poor, naked Christ. Joined by others who had heard a similar call, he took up the role of evangelist for the Gospel to revive and reform the established church. Pope Innocent III perceived, after some persuasion by Francis, that these "little brothers" or Friars Minor could serve as an instrument for communicating the Word of God, promoting peace, and cultivating goodness; they could call the church to penance and a life of holiness through the poverty of their lifestyle and the simplicity of their speech, a performance of the "Gospel Life."[4] As Francis wrote in the Order's Earlier Rule, the *Regula non bullata* of 1221, "This is the life of the Gospel of Jesus Christ which Brother Francis asked the Lord Pope to be granted and confirmed for him." The rule and life of these "little brothers" was simply this: "to live in obedience, in chastity, and without anything of their own, and to follow the teaching and the footprints of the Lord Jesus Christ."[5]

This new movement, however, clearly defined itself and its mission within the authorized faith and practices of the established church while still enjoying certain freedoms extended by the papal office. In Chapter 17, "On Preachers," Francis wrote, "No brother shall preach contrary to

3. Jacques Le Goff, *Saint Francis of Assisi*, trans. Christine Rhone (New York: Routledge, 2004), pp. 29-30.

4. Lawrence S. Cunningham, *Francis of Assisi: Performing the Gospel Life* (Grand Rapids: Eerdmans, 2004), p. 134. I am indebted to Cunningham's excellent introduction to Francis.

5. *Francis and Clare: The Complete Works*, trans. Regis J. Armstrong, O.F.M., and Ignatius C. Brady, O.F.M. (New York: Paulist Press, 1982), pp. 108-9.

the form and regulations of the holy church nor unless he has been permitted by his minister."[6] At the same time, the brothers were summoned to preach always by their deeds. No regular minister or preacher, however, was permitted to appropriate to himself the ministry of the brothers or the office of preaching, but was to set aside the office of preaching without any protest whenever so ordered by ecclesial authority.

The substance and scope of this preaching was prescribed by Francis in the Later Rule, the *Regula Bullata* of 1223, where he wrote in Chapter 9, "On Preachers," "I also admonish and exhort these brothers that, in their preaching, their words be well chosen and chaste for the instruction and edification of the people, speaking to them of vices and virtues, punishment and glory in a discourse that is brief, because it was in a few words that the Lord preached while on earth."[7] This way of preaching was founded on the Gospel and embodied its humble style — *sermo humilis*. For Francis, preaching therefore aimed at transmitting the words of Jesus Christ, who is the Word of the Father, and the words of the Holy Ghost that are Spirit and Life. Moreover, in keeping with the Gospel story of Jesus, this preaching tended to take place outside the church, in town squares, in homes, on roadsides — wherever there were people. Such humble preaching created its own space, transforming public space into the space of the word of salvation. This was a form of homiletic activity that "reveled in narrative, emotion, and in the commonplace, and that was focused on a very human Christ both in his Incarnation and in the mystery of his passion."[8]

Until and beyond his death, the character and charisma of Francis remained stamped on the life of the order.

Bonaventure, Heir of Saint Francis

Francis's most important successor was arguably Bonaventure of Bagnorea (d. 1274), who served as general minister from 1257 to 1274 and was considered to be the second founder of the Franciscan Order. Bonaventure's primary challenge was both to preserve and to reinterpret the spirit of Francis

---

6. *Francis and Clare*, pp. 122-23.
7. *Francis and Clare*, p. 143.
8. Le Goff, *Saint Francis of Assisi*, pp. 117-20, here p. 118; Cunningham, *Francis of Assisi*, pp. 41-42, 34-36.

while holding radical and fundamentalist members in check. Moreover, by this time the office of preaching was clericalized among the brothers so that its purpose was conversion of life and repentance; the full effect of the sermon was its completion in sacramental confession.[9] As Franciscan General Minister, Bonaventure addressed this change by describing the virtues required of those called to serve in pastoral leadership. In *The Character of a Christian Leader*, an interpretation of the Six Seraphs of Isaiah 6:2, he discussed zeal for righteousness, brotherly love, patience, an exemplary life, discretion, and devotion to God, providing models of each virtue from Scripture and the Christian tradition.[10]

In 1260, Bonaventure was authorized to write a biography, the *Legendarium*, the *Life of St. Francis*, which not only completed several previous similar works but also provided a fresh interpretation of Franciscan spirituality within the context of Bonaventure's theology as a whole. The *Legendarium* is organized thematically to describe Francis's conversion, the founding and spread of the Order, Francis's practice of the Gospel virtues, poverty, obedience, and purity, and the three stages of the spiritual life: purgation, illumination, and perfection.[11] Significantly, Bonaventure includes a chapter entitled "On the Efficacy of His Preaching and His Grace of Healing," in which the words of Francis reveal the necessity of both contemplative and active forms of life, devotion to prayer, and the practice of preaching — listening to God and speaking to humanity:

> What do you think, brothers, what do you judge better, that I should spend my time in prayer, or that I should go about preaching? I am a poor little man, simple and unskilled in speech, I have received a greater grace of prayer than of speaking. Also in prayer there seems to be a profit and the accumulative of graces, but in preaching the distribution of gifts already received from heaven. . . . Finally, in prayer we address God, listen to him and dwell among the angels as if we were

9. Lawrence, *The Friars*, pp. 43-64; *Rooted in Faith: Homilies to a Contemporary World by St. Bonaventure*, trans. Marigwen Schumacher (Chicago: Franciscan Herald Press, 1974), pp. xvii-xxvii; Southern, *Western Society and the Church in the Middle Ages*, pp. 279-90; McGinn, *The Presence of God*, vol. 3: *The Flowering of Mysticism*, pp. 70-112.

10. Bonaventure, *The Character of a Christian Leader: Originally Titled "The Six Wings of the Seraph,"* trans. Philip O'Mara (Ann Arbor, Mich.: Servant Books, 1978).

11. *Bonaventure: The Soul's Journey into God, The Tree of Life, The Life of St. Francis*, trans. Ewert Cousins (New York: Paulist Press, 1978), pp. 177-328.

living an angelic life; in preaching we must think, see, say, and hear human things, adapting ourselves to them as if we were living on a human level, for men among men.[12]

In addition to the *Legendarium*, Francis inspired what is arguably Bonaventure's greatest piece, the *Itinerarium mentis in Deum (The Soul's Journey into God)*, which is a speculative, mystical treatise whose central theme came to him while he was meditating at Mount La Verna in Tuscany on the vision of the six-winged Seraphim in the form of the Crucified — an experience that Francis had had at the same spot in 1224. The work is a dense *summa* of Christian spirituality that expresses the essence and spirit of Francis's life and vision as perceived by Bonaventure. *The Soul's Journey into God* articulates the Franciscan awareness of God's presence in creation and Francis's joy in the beauty and sacramental nature of everything God has made. These gifts, however, are closely linked with devotion to the humanity of Christ and love for Christ Incarnate so as to interpret material creation as manifesting God, the Word. This is the beginning of a journey toward a kind of passionate, spiritual knowledge of the Trinity, guided by divine illumination and constituted by sensible, psychological, and metaphysical stages of contemplation.[13]

This vision of spiritual theology, or theology as a spiritual vocation, is significant for understanding Bonaventure's manner of reading and preaching Scripture, since his theology was experiential, an awareness of God given through Christ and the Spirit, at once both knowledge and love that are the cause and effect of transformation, which is wisdom. Spiritual progress is therefore an integral part of theology, an entire way of life that starts from the original condition of humanity and its fall, but with the help of the Word and Spirit, returns and culminates in the new creation in Jesus Christ.[14] Theology, and its expression through preach-

---

12. Bonaventure, *The Soul's Journey into God, The Tree of Life, The Life of St. Francis*, pp. 291-92.

13. See the Introduction by Cousins in Bonaventure, *The Soul's Journey into God, The Tree of Life, The Life of St. Francis*, pp. 18-34; J. A. Wayne Hellman, "The Spirituality of the Franciscans," in *Christian Spirituality: High Middle Ages and Reformation*, ed. Jill Raitt, in collaboration with Bernard McGinn and John Meyendorff (New York: Crossroad, 2001), pp. 41-44; Diogenes Allen, *Spiritual Theology* (Boston: Cowley Publications, 1997), pp. 110-16; McGinn, *The Presence of God*, vol. 3: *The Flowering of Mysticism*, pp. 87-93.

14. McGinn, *The Presence of God*, vol. 3: *The Flowering of Mysticism*, pp. 91-92.

ing, is pursued from a perspective acquired through prayerful study of sacred Scripture and the theological virtues of faith, hope, and love; its object is Christ Crucified, who purifies the theologian and preacher for personal union with him. For Bonaventure, therefore, "theology is sapiential, the love of God that results in a *habitus,* an affective disposition that is wisdom, the road or way that leads to holiness through the sanctifying grace and gifts of the Spirit."[15]

The Breviloquium: *Theology and Scripture*

A primary example of Bonaventure's vision of theology is the Prologue to the *Breviloquium,* which he wrote to provide beginning students with a brief exposition of all that is vital and significant in the Christian faith, a systematic approach to the love of God that integrates the passion of a mystic and the logic of a theologian.[16] The theme of theology is simply God and God as First Principle; theology is the study of sacred Scripture as illumined by the Fathers; divine wisdom from God, of God, according to God, for and to God as its end. The purpose of theology, therefore, is that we become virtuous and attain salvation, which is accomplished by an inclination of the will ordered to the love of God rather than through philosophical speculation. According to Bonaventure, the study of sacred doctrine — sacred Scripture — lovingly attends to the Triune God and comprises seven topics: the Creation of the World, the Corruption of Sin, the Incarnation of the Word, the Grace of the Holy Spirit, the Sacramental Remedy, and the Last Stage or Final Judgment.

The Prologue to the *Breviloquium* is based on Ephesians 3:14-19, from which Bonaventure draws his understanding of the origin, development, and end of sacred Scripture, which is analogous to the attributes of God's love revealed in Christ and acclaimed by the Apostle Paul, "great teacher of the nations and preacher of the Truth." Sacred Scripture originated under the influence of the Holy Trinity and was developed according to human capacity; because its end consists in the superabundance of over-

15. Charles Carpenter, *Theology as the Road to Holiness in St. Bonaventure* (New York: Paulist Press, 2001), pp. 13-36.

16. *The Works of St. Bonaventure: Cardinal Seraphic Doctor and Saint,* vol. 2: *The Breviloquium,* trans. José de Vinck (Paterson, N.J.: St. Anthony Guild Press, 1963); Aidan Nichols, O.P., *The Shape of Catholic Theology: An Introduction to Its Sources, Principles, and History* (Collegeville, Minn.: Liturgical Press, 1991), p. 172.

flowing happiness, it cannot be understood without knowledge of Jesus Christ, faith in whom is the lamp, door, and foundation of all scriptural wisdom. Such knowledge is a gift of the Blessed Trinity, an inspired provision for a wayfaring humanity in its journey toward the fullness of the divine gift of salvation.

According to Bonaventure, Scripture in its literal and figurative language sums up the content of the entire universe, describes the whole course of history, displays the glory of the saved, recounts the misery of the reprobate, and reveals the depth of God's judgment. Scripture's content and properties thus reflect the glory of humanity; Scripture mirrors the complex reality of the whole created world, thereby meeting the demands of human understanding and restoring creation toward the knowledge, love, and praise of God:

> And so the whole course of the universe is shown by the Scriptures to run in a most orderly fashion from beginning to end, like a beautifully composed poem in which every mind may discover, through the succession of events, the diversity, multiplicity, and justice, the order, rectitude, and beauty, of the countless divine decrees that produce from God's ruling the universe. But as no one can appreciate the beauty of a poem unless his vision embraces the whole, so no one can see the beauty of the orderly governance of the creation unless he has an integral view of it.[17]

Salvation is therefore attained only by those who travel the "straight road of Scripture," a journey that requires always beginning at the beginning with the same spirit of pure faith, knowing and living Christ, which is demonstrated by the lives of the Saints. Moreover, God, in Christ and the Holy Spirit, speaks through the mouths of the biblical writers when they are read according to the church's rule of faith, in accord with Christian belief and practice.[18] Illuminating the intellect and drawing the will by means of Scripture's deeds and words, the Spirit takes up the book of creation, the story of history and its final end, by means of its senses: what to believe, what to do, and what to hope for. Guided by divine wisdom,

17. *The Works of St. Bonaventure: Breviloquium*, pp. 11-12.
18. Joseph P. Wawrykow, "Reflections on the Place of the *De doctrina Christiana* in High Scholastic Discussions of Theology," in *Reading and Wisdom: The "De doctrina Christiana" of Augustine in the Middle Ages*, ed. Edward D. English (Notre Dame: University of Notre Dame Press, 1995), p. 113.

Scripture's teaching bears fruit in the cultivation of virtuous deeds, luminous faith, and ardent love for God.[19]

Bonaventure the Preacher

Bonaventure's homiletic practice was informed by the theological exegesis of Scripture, which for him meant that preacher and people are taken up into the activity of God, who speaks through Scripture to effect human salvation. His sermons were therefore concerned with Scripture itself, the doctrine it contains, as well as discovering, reflecting upon, and expounding its truths. For this fundamental reason, he believed that the preacher must first of all learn to be a devout listener: the origin of divine speech is the Triune God; sacred Scripture is the "heart, mouth, tongue and pen of God."[20]

Bonaventure thus integrated the tasks of exegesis, teaching, and preaching to the end that salvation, in its fullness, might be received, take root, and return the faithful to God. Scripture's content proceeds from God himself, which makes it worthy of the listener's faithful acceptance and assent. Moreover, Scripture's message is authentic, since it bears the authority of God, who creates a fundamental relationship between Christ the Redeemer and the redeeming quality of the Bible, thereby authorizing human speech illumined by faith, hope, and love. Bonaventure's sacramental vision of the saving activity of the Divine Word speaking is exemplified by his sermon entitled "Gospel for the Fifth Sunday after the Epiphany": "The Kingdom of heaven may be compared to a man who sowed good seed in his field" (Matt. 13:24).[21]

---

19. *The Works of St. Bonaventure: Breviloquium*, pp. 1-32. See the thorough discussion of Bonaventure's theology in Carpenter, *Theology as the Road to Holiness in St. Bonaventure*. See also Thomas Reist, O.F.M., Conv., *Saint Bonaventure as a Biblical Commentator: A Translation and Analysis of His Commentary on Luke, XVIII,34–XIX,42* (Lanham, Md.: University Press of America, 1985), pp. 29-47; McGinn, *The Presence of God*, vol. 3: *The Flowering of Mysticism*, pp. 102-4.

20. Cited in Michael Robson, "Saint Bonaventure," in *The Medieval Theologians: An Introduction to Theology in the Medieval Period*, ed. G. R. Evans (Oxford: Blackwell, 1991), p. 188. On Bonaventure's preaching, see Reist, *Saint Bonaventure as a Biblical Commentator*, pp. 174-80; Timothy J. Johnson, *Bonaventure: Mystic of God's Word* (Hyde Park, N.Y.: New City Press, 1999), pp. 10-26, 47-49, 73-75, 137-39; *What Manner of Man: Sermons on Christ by St. Bonaventure*, trans. Zachary Hays, O.F.M. (Chicago: Franciscan Herald Press, 1974), pp. 3-13.

21. Johnson, *Bonaventure: Mystic of God's Word*, pp. 75-82; hereafter cited parenthetically in the text as *MGW*.

The introductory remarks, which serve to engage and orient the audience, presumably students and friars, draw from Sirach 48:1: "Then Elijah arose, a prophet burning like fire, and his word blazed like a torch." Bonaventure draws from his reading of Sirach to offer several senses of the "preaching life." The preacher must rise above carnal-mindedness ("Then Elijah arose"); the preacher must be inflamed with charity for the salvation of all people ("burning like fire"); and the preacher must, through a holy manner of life, be resplendent, shedding light on the minds of others ("his word blazed like a torch") (MGW, 75).

Bonaventure confesses that he has fallen short on all three counts, but he implores his listeners to invoke the tender compassion of God so that his words might serve the glory of God and the salvation of souls. His primary homiletic aim is to expose the truth of the text spoken by Christ to illumine sight-impaired humanity, that is, "the marvelous work of the creation of humankind through the apt metaphor of a man sowing seed in his field." According to Bonaventure, the sowing activity of God in the world originates with the creation of humankind. The metaphor of sowing captures the several dimensions of this creation: its operative principle, through the image of humanity; its receptive subject, through the symbol of the field; the intermediate act, through the sowing of good seed. Bonaventure then identifies the operative principle of creation, "The Kingdom of heaven may be compared to a man," as speaking of God. The receptive subject is his field, the world, while the intermediate act is inferred from the words "sowed good seed," since God created humankind according to the divine image and likeness (MGW, 76).

These three distinctions are expounded to illumine the creative power, wisdom, and goodness of God, and to display the origin, means and end of humanity, the world, the conscience, and heaven. Bonaventure's exposition of the parable, therefore, is a demonstration of the integral relationship of these three points, or movements, that disclose the supernatural power of God who creates the whole universe. In addition, divine wisdom orders all things harmoniously through preaching to overcome vice and cultivate virtue, and to bring the consummation of justice and mercy, creation's final end, either the reward of glory or the punishment of the wicked (MGW, 77-78).

The concluding part of the sermon recapitulates the earlier themes, re-emphasizing that God sows the good seed of both spiritual and material substances in the world; that God governs the conscience with wisdom, heavenly influences, and the perfected existence of grace; and that God is the Goodness who draws all things to their completion in the heavenly homeland. Bonaventure's plain but vividly imaginative exposition calls his listeners to receive the Word of God sown in their midst, to hear the Word with reverence and understanding, to put its truth into practice, becoming themselves the good soil that bears much fruit. The sermon closes with a strong note of hope: God's goodness, which draws all creatures to their heavenly destiny, has already sown the splendor that bestows the fulfilled existence of glory. Shining with the presence of divine beauty, Bonaventure's listeners are that seed, those whom the Lord has blessed with the beatitude of glory and clothed with the garments of salvation (*MGW*, 81-82).

Bonaventure's homiletic aim was simply to be an instrument of the divine seed, God's Word, sown in the words of Christ speaking through the parable, and the words of the preacher speaking through the sermon. As the Word of God, Scripture's message cannot be separated from the speech of its human agents, since its authority encompasses both divine and human activity within the economy of creation and redemption. Thus a larger theological vision informs Bonaventure's understanding of divine causality in the work of salvation. The efficient cause of the Bible, divine efficacy, is the source of his confidence that, in the activity of preaching, he and his listeners are graced participants in the movement of God to humanity by means of Scripture's teaching: sacred doctrine.[22] Most significant for Bonaventure is that the saving knowledge and love of God — divine wisdom — originates entirely with the Triune God, and that this wisdom is disclosed in the history of God's dealings with the world as focused in Jesus Christ (*MGW*, 83).

Collations on the Ten Commandments

During the season of Lent in 1267, Bonaventure delivered his *Collations on the Ten Commandments* at the University of Paris, a collection of talks that demonstrates how his unified reading of Scripture centered on Jesus

22. See the excellent discussion on medieval views of scriptural causality that allow for both divine and human freedom and activity in Christopher Ocker, *Biblical Poetics before Humanism and Reformation* (Cambridge: Cambridge University Press, 2002).

Christ and the Trinity.[23] According to Bonaventure, both the Old and the New Testaments are divided in a fourfold manner: legal, historical, sapiential, and prophetical. The Old is contained in the New, and vice versa. His interpretation therefore expresses the Christian fulfillment of prophecy in the economy of salvation.[24]

This vision of Scripture enabled Bonaventure to read the Decalogue according to the words of Christ, the Great Teacher who both commands and authorizes faithful obedience: "If you wish to enter into life, keep the commandments." Moreover, the words of Jesus reveal the entire substance of salvation and human action. Because the "end moves the agent," both preachers and listeners must learn to desire what they see and hear; scriptural precepts are to be internalized for public enactment.

Bonaventure's reading divides the commandments according to the Great Commandment of Matthew 22: according to Christ, they reveal the rule of divine justice, which is ordered to love of God and love of neighbor. The First Table contains those commandments that order our life to God. These are three, since God is Triune — Father, Son, and Holy Spirit, to whom are attributed majesty, truth, and goodness. The Second Table contains seven commandments, which order our lives to neighbors and contain the natural law, which requires that we do unto others as we wish they would do unto us.[25]

Bonaventure's theological interpretation of the Ten Commandments may be read as a *summa* of the Christian life; wisdom for a pilgrim people journeying toward salvation; pastoral teaching that flows from the proper adoration of the Father, confession of the Son, and love for the Holy Spirit. In the final collation, Bonaventure reveals the purpose of his teaching: "Now from the observance of the Law a person becomes respectful, fruitful, devout, pious, meek, chaste, generous, truthful, content with his own things, of a generous heart and pure mind." These virtues are made possible, however, by the liberating work of Christ, since

23. *St. Bonaventure's Collations on the Ten Commandments*, trans. Paul J. Spaeth, ed. F. Edward Coughlin, O.F.M. (St. Bonaventure, N.Y.: The Franciscan Institute, 1995). See Spaeth's introduction, pp. 1-16.

24. *The Works of St. Bonaventure: Breviloquium*, pp. 1-22. On the four senses of Scripture, see Bonaventure, "Collations on the Six Days: Thirteenth Collation," in *Theories of Preaching: Selected Readings in the Homiletical Tradition*, ed. Richard Lischer (Durham, N.C.: The Labyrinth Press, 1987), pp. 145-47.

25. *St. Bonaventure's Collations on the Ten Commandments*, pp. 25-28.

through him God has overcome the ten plagues, lifting humanity from death to life and from darkness to light. On the basis of Christ's finished work, Bonaventure offers a final exhortation: "Therefore, we must rise up to new life. . . . Christ has liberated us this time from the hand of Pharaoh and has led us into the promised-land."[26]

Thomas Aquinas: Exemplar of the Dominicans

Historical Context

In addition to the Franciscans, the Order of Friars Preachers, the Dominicans, were also founded during the thirteenth-century upsurge of evangelical fervor that pressed for the renewal of the church from within and without official ecclesial sanctions and structures. In the case of the Dominicans, founder Dominic of Guzman (1170-1221) was deeply involved in 1206 with preaching Christian doctrine against dualism, the heretical teaching of the Albigensians and Cathars, while en route through southern France with his bishop Diego, of Osma, Spain.[27]

These heterodox groups, who were winning converts through their preaching, pastoral care, and ascetic way of life, presented serious challenges to Catholic doctrine and practice that revealed the need for a well-informed and devoted clergy, made all the more pressing by the emergence of an increasingly articulate, critical laity. Dominic's personal, intellectually rigorous response to these heretical groups, his holy preaching, was the inspiration for the founding of the Dominicans as an order dedicated to the apostolic life, embodied in a style of itinerant, mendicant preaching that took priority over all other spiritual practices, even prayer and the celebration of the sacraments.[28] Pierre Mandonnet writes,

26. *St. Bonaventure's Collations on the Ten Commandments,* pp. 96-101.

27. C. H. Lawrence, *Medieval Monasticism* (New York: Longman, 1984), pp. 193-210. For a description of twelfth- and thirteenth-century heresies, see Malcolm Lambert, *Medieval Heresy: Popular Movements from the Gregorian Reform to the Reformation* (Oxford: Blackwell, 1992), pp. 35-146.

28. Allan White, O.P., "The Foundation of the Order of Preachers and Its Historical Setting," in *The Way of the Preacher,* ed. Simon Tugwell, O.P. (London: Darton, Longman & Todd Ltd., 1979), pp. 97-110. See also Nicholas M. Healy, *Thomas Aquinas: Theologian of the Christian Life* (Burlington, Vt.: Ashgate Publishing, 2003), pp. 1-14, 24-33; "Introduction," in

The founding of the Order of Friars Preachers was very closely bound up with the general needs that were making themselves felt in the Christian world at the start of the thirteenth century. Having encouraged religious life in this new stage of development, the church of Rome decided to make use of it in order to solve some of the urgent problems confronting the church. . . . The ministry needed an ecclesial militia that was both well-educated and directly in contact with the social life of the times. The Friars preachers with their new type of religious life and original mode of organization were the answer to the needs of the new age.[29]

The Dominicans, therefore, were a movement of traveling preachers, vowed to imitate what they pictured as Jesus' simple life of traveling ministry according to the formula of Luke 10, in contrast to the stability of noble families, rich merchants, and settled monasteries. In 1216 the order was approved as an Order of Preachers not confined to any single diocese and not dependent on any bishop for its mandate to preach. The Dominicans were not simply people who were available to preach when needed; they, by right and by definition, were preachers.

Sharing in the agitations and miseries of growing cities and urban dwellers, the Dominicans sought to embody the apostolic and missionary dimensions of the Gospel and the Christian life by combining serious study, imitation of Jesus, commitment to poverty, and dependence on the grace of the Holy Spirit for the work of evangelization and catechetical preaching. Joining the ministry of the Word of God to that of hearing confessions, the brothers shared the vocation of the "preaching life," a spirituality that embodied a theological and pastoral vision of a community united with Christ and motivated by the virtue of charity. The brothers were organized and sent out by Dominic for a mission that would eventually extend throughout and even beyond the boundaries of Christendom. What stands out most of all is a zeal for the salvation of souls, as directed by the *Primitive Constitutions*, charter documents of the Dominican way of life:

Early Dominicans: Selected Writings, ed. Simon Tugwell, O.P. (New York: Paulist Press, 1982), pp. 1-48; Southern, *Western Society and the Church in the Middle Ages*, pp. 279-84.

29. Cited in Thomas O'Meara, O.P., *Thomas Aquinas: Theologian* (Notre Dame: University of Notre Dame Press, 1997), p. 6.

They shall set forth and shall everywhere comport themselves as men who seek to obtain their own salvation and that of their neighbor, in all perfection and the spirit of religion; like evangelical men following in the footsteps of their Saviour, speaking with God and of God, either with themselves or with their neighbors. . . . When they thus set forth to exercise the ministry of preaching, or to travel for any other reason, they are not to receive or carry any gold, silver, or coin or any other gift except food, clothing, and other necessary equipment, and books.[30]

The Dominicans, then, were identified by their central activity: preaching. It was the fruit of prayerful study and contemplation, and was motivated by the gift of divine charity, a generous outpouring of human speech in union with the Word of God, active in creation and redemption and incarnate in Jesus Christ.[31]

However, by 1254 the movement was in crisis. That year, Humbert of Romans was elected Master of the Order, assuming leadership during a time when the mendicants were under attack because of their break with the established monastic way of life, their itinerant ministry, and their exclusive accountability to papal authority. Perhaps Humbert's greatest contribution during this time of crisis was his treatise *On the Formation of Preachers,* which ascribed an even cosmic significance to preaching and provided an authoritative statement about what it might mean to structure the life of the Dominicans around this vocation.[32]

The most significant characteristic of Humbert's treatise is its strangeness. It fits neither into the familiar model of medieval spiritual literature nor into the increasingly popular genre of the "art of preaching" that is more concerned with the techniques and technicalities of preparing, designing, and delivering sermons. Instead, Humbert offers an alternative form of writing that addresses both the identity and the activity of the preaching life and its most important element: that preachers are called and taught by God.[33] What has to be discerned is the "grace of

---

30. *Early Dominicans,* ed. Tugwell, p. 467.

31. *The Way of the Preacher,* ed. Tugwell, pp. 82-96.

32. "Treatise on the Formation of Preachers," in *Early Dominicans,* ed. Tugwell, pp. 179-355; hereafter cited parenthetically in the text as "TFP."

33. See the survey in Phyllis B. Roberts, "The *Ars Praedicandi* and the Medieval Sermon," in *Preacher, Sermon, and Audience in the Middle Ages,* ed. Carolyn Muessig (Leiden: Brill, 2002), pp. 41-62.

preaching," which is the crucial factor, since what makes preaching different from a lecture, a speech, or a form of cultural entertainment is the dimension of grace, which must enter and affect both preachers' and listeners' lives. Despite the Dominicans' success, Humbert recognized that ultimately, though hard work, training, and talent all matter, it is the Holy Spirit who teaches the "art of preaching."[34]

The *Formation of Preachers*, therefore, was written to cultivate practical wisdom and judgment for the preaching life. The treatise covers seven topics: the characteristics of the job, what a preacher needs to do the job, right and wrong ways of taking the job, the actual performance of the job, ways in which people come to be without preaching, the results of preaching, and things that go with the job of preaching ("TFP," 183). The enduring value of the work is its wealth of insights, personalized reflections, and prescient observations from the pen of a master preacher.

Significantly, Humbert begins in a theological manner by highlighting the divinely bestowed nobility of preaching: it is an apostolic, angelic, and divine task that God became man to do. The nobility of preaching is affirmed by the status of Scripture, the source of its content and purpose. Moreover, Scripture is the highest of sciences; it speaks of exalted matters such as the Trinity and the Incarnation and seeks to acquire eternal life for preachers and listeners by means of divine wisdom, which points to God himself. Humbert asserts, "That is why sacred scripture is referred to as 'theology' from *Theos* (God) and *logos* (Word), because its words are from God, about God and directed to God." Moreover, it is God who calls and sends preachers to speak a living word to a dying world: "just as God will, at the end of time, raise up dead bodies by his word, so he now gives life to dead spirits by the power of his word" ("TFP," 184-85).

According to Humbert, preaching is not so easily learned in comparison with other arts, such as building or playing a musical instrument. The success of preaching must be attributed to God's special gift and empowerment, the grace or pedagogy of the Holy Spirit, since the Word of God must govern human speech. On the other hand, the preacher must work diligently, with the aid of grace, to commend himself through devotion to study, imitation of wise exemplars, and frequent prayer, thereby

---

34. Tugwell, *Early Dominicans*, pp. 181-82. See the excellent discussion on the grace of preaching in Tugwell, *The Way of the Preacher*, pp. 33-41.

discerning what is prudent for the conversion and edification of others ("TFP," 205-10).

A preacher must therefore possess goodness of life, characterized by a holy conscience, a reputation beyond reproof, austerity, public witness, integrity of words and actions, and an attractive manner. In addition, certain forms of knowledge are also needed: knowledge of Holy Scripture, which is taught by God; knowledge of creatures and the divine wisdom they reveal; knowledge of stories, both Christian and secular; knowledge of Christian doctrine; knowledge of the mysteries of the church; knowledge of practical matters; knowledge of prudence or good sense; and most important, knowledge of the Holy Spirit. Moreover, a preacher also must speak fluently and possess a facility with words, in addition to having a strong, clear voice, the ability to preach with clarity and coherence, and the good sense to speak different things to different people. Above all, he must have "graciousness upon the lips" ("TFP," 215-24).

Above everything else, if the Word is to be heard properly, it must be spoken and received with joy, desire, persistence, care, reverence, attention, passion, patience, and devotion. For in the end the Word must not only be heard, it must be enacted: preacher and people must devote all their available energy to living what is proclaimed ("TFP," 269-80).

As the discussion of Humbert's work suggests, the Dominicans' education and practice were committed to doctrinal preaching, which was reserved for the clergy and required the necessary intellectual training. The integration of intellectual preparation and imitation of the apostolic life came to characterize the Order of Friars Preachers. It equipped its preachers to respond in both a theological and a pastoral manner to new intellectual challenges and the threat of heresies, while embodying a flexible, evangelical way of life motivated by charity and a desire to communicate the truth of Christian teaching. Study, therefore, "was a matter of life and death."[35]

The early Dominican constitutions exemplify the order's approach: carefully examining its preachers to determine what grace of preaching they possessed, and inquiring about habits of study, religious life, depth of charity, commitment, and intention. Preachers who displayed suffi-

---

35. Southern, *Western Society and the Church in the Middle Ages*, p. 299. Also see Simon Tugwell, "The Spirituality of the Dominicans," in *Christian Spirituality: High Middle Ages and Reformation*, pp. 15-25.

cient evidence in these areas were deployed, while others were assigned to further study and practice under the supervision of more experienced brothers.[36] While study was not the end of the order, it was necessary to secure its end, namely preaching and the salvation of souls, for without study neither could be accomplished.[37]

Thomas Aquinas, "Master of the Sacred Page"

Best known among the Dominican Masters was Thomas Aquinas (d. 1274).[38] Within the biblical culture cultivated by the Franciscans and the Dominicans, Aquinas bore the title Master of the Sacred Page, *magister in sacra pagina*, which refers to the entire effort of bearing witness to the revelation of the Word of God mediated through sacred Scripture. His life and work as a member of the Order of Preachers demonstrates how the intellectual love of God, undertaken with full seriousness, can itself be a genuine form of piety, provided it is motivated by charity, and especially if it is also motivated by a desire to communicate the truth of God to other people. In thirteenth-century terms, Aquinas's task was threefold: *legere, disputare, predicare* — to comment on, to dispute doctrinal questions, and to preach before both academic and popular audiences. These responsibilities were defined in the context of apostolic ministry, where all three functions arose from the profession of theology, *theologia*, or sacred doctrine, *sacra doctrina* — the knowledge and love of God.[39] However, according to Marie Dominique Chenu,

> These tasks . . . were not distinct disciplines as in modern practice; they were all seen as parts of a more or less unified theological program of articulating, shaping, and embodying convictions about God, human-

36. Tugwell, *Early Dominicans*, pp. 466-67.

37. Southern, *Western Society and the Church in the Middle Ages*, pp. 298-99.

38. See the excellent introduction in *Albert and Thomas: Selected Writings*, trans. and ed. Simon Tugwell, O.P. (Mahwah, N.J.: Paulist Press, 1988), pp. 201-352. See also the discussions of Aquinas in Jean-Pierre Torrell, O.P., *Saint Thomas Aquinas*, trans. Robert Royal, 2 vols. (Washington, D.C.: Catholic University Press, 1996-2003); Healy, *Thomas Aquinas: Theologian of the Christian Life*; O'Meara, *Thomas Aquinas: Theologian*; Aidan Nichols, O.P., *Discovering Aquinas: An Introduction to His Life, Work, and Influence* (Grand Rapids: Eerdmans, 2002); Fergus Kerr, O.P., *After Aquinas: Versions of Thomism* (London: Blackwell, 2002); Marie Dominique Chenu, O.P., *Aquinas and His Role in Theology* (Collegeville, Minn.: Liturgical Press, 2002).

39. Torrell, *Saint Thomas Aquinas*, 1:4-74; 2:1-24.

ity, and the world in order to communicate and nurture Christian wisdom. This ensemble of theological practices — exegetical, dogmatic, and pastoral in nature — were personally integrated within a sapiential vision shaped by the Gospel; each of these required a receptivity, transmission, and participation evoked by the active presence of the Word and the operation of the Holy Spirit for its realization in the life of the church and the salvation of the world.[40]

The Summa Theologiae: *Theology for Preachers*

The most important work Thomas produced was the *Summa Theologiae*, which must be viewed within the context of his vocation as a Dominican, his study of Scripture and the Fathers, and his commitment to the order's principles of obedience, poverty, and preaching.[41] The purpose of the *Summa* was to prepare Dominicans, both beginners and advanced students, to interpret Scripture and dispute doctrinal matters in performing their vocation of preaching, teaching, and living the Gospel more truly in following the way of Jesus Christ. Thus Thomas's concept of *sacra doctrina*, holy teaching, reflects and continues Dominic's original commitment to the mission of *sancta praedicatia*, holy preaching.[42]

The overall narrative movement of the *Summa* depends upon Scripture for its order, going from God, to creatures, and then to Christ, through whom all creatures return to God. From first to last it is a narrative of the Word spoken that breathes forth Love. The *Prima Pars* deals with God, who is both One and Triune in himself as the source and goal of all creation. The *Secunda Pars* deals specifically with practical theology, the study of the Christian life: the drama of conversion and true discipleship, the virtues and vices, the narrative of human beings called to achieve their fulfillment in God by the exercise of freedom under the

---

40. Chenu, *Aquinas and His Role in Theology*, pp. 20-31.

41. Thomas Aquinas, *Summa Theologiae*, trans. Fathers of the English Dominican Province (Westminster, Md.: Christian Classics, 1981); hereafter cited parenthetically in the text as *ST*.

42. Leonard Boyle, O.P., *The Setting of the "Summa Theologiae" of Thomas Aquinas* (Toronto: Pontifical Institute of Medieval Studies, 1981); Healy, *Thomas Aquinas: Theologian of the Christian Life*, pp. 28-48; Nichols, *Discovering Aquinas*, pp. 9-18; Kerr, *After Aquinas*, pp. 117-19. See also the excellent discussion of the *Summa* and its use in John I. Jenkins, C.S.C., *Knowledge and Faith in Thomas Aquinas* (Cambridge: Cambridge University Press, 2001).

guidance and grace of God. The *Tertia Pars* provides the climax of the whole work in Christ, the Son of God, the Incarnation and the sacramental life of the church through the grace of the Spirit.[43]

"The first two parts of the *Summa* can therefore be seen as an elaborate statement of the *dramatis personae*, God and ourselves, with a supporting cast of other creatures."[44] This drama consists in the bringing together of God and us in beatitude, the happiness of eternal life, and it centers on Jesus Christ, who is both the model and the objective foundation for our movement toward God, who is himself the Way by which we come to union with God. It is by means of the practices of the church, through constancy in its worship and sacramental life, that its members enter upon and process along this Way. Acquiring the requisite knowledge and dispositions — faith, hope, and love — is necessary to participate in the narrative of creation and redemption revealed in Scripture and explicated in the authoritative tradition of its interpretation.[45] "Thus the *Summa* is actually no more than a series of 'grammatical' notes upon the reading of Scripture, being entirely determined by the scriptural story of the world redeemed in Christ."[46]

Christian faith, which rests on no other foundation than the revelation made to the Prophets and the Apostles, is depicted as a practice that embraces both thinking and living; the *Summa* thus integrates the spirituality of monastic culture with the intellectual pursuit of the universities. According to Thomas, God has destined humanity for a union with himself: "Man's whole salvation, which is in God, depends upon knowledge of this truth." Faith thus adheres to the articles of faith and reason on the basis of the Creed, which is the summary of sacred Scripture, and through which First Truth (God speaking) is mediated through the church's diverse practices of holy teaching according to its intellectual tradition (*ST* 1A.1.2).[47]

---

43. Torrell, *Saint Thomas Aquinas*, pp. 25-52; Nichols, *Discovering Aquinas*, pp. 9-13.

44. Tugwell, *Albert and Thomas*, p. 257.

45. Kerr, *After Aquinas*, pp. 162-67.

46. Gerard Loughlin, "The Basis and Authority of Doctrine," in *The Cambridge Companion to Christian Doctrine*, ed. Colin Gunton (Cambridge: Cambridge University Press, 1997), pp. 45-57; here, p. 45.

47. For an excellent discussion of sacred doctrine or holy teaching, see R. Francis Martin, "*Sacra Doctrina* and the Authority of Its *Sacra Scriptura*," *Pro Ecclesia* 10, no. 1 (2000): 84-102; Jaroslav Pelikan, *Credo: Historical and Theological Guide to Creeds and Confessions of Faith in the Christian Tradition* (New Haven: Yale University Press, 2003), pp. 444-45.

For Thomas, then, theological activity is not so much a human task as a divine self-giving, one of the primary ways in which human creatures are drawn into the life revealed by God. The communicative dimension of sacred doctrine, of which God is the principal agent, and the preaching and teaching of Scripture as its primary form must be seen as a *habitus*, a disposition, a consequence of spiritual transformation through which the preacher, having received the gift of divine wisdom mediated through the Word and grace of the Holy Spirit, becomes a participant in God's own knowledge and love.[48] Anna Williams sums up the goal of Thomas's spiritual pedagogy: "We do not speak in order that others might be persuaded; we speak because we have been transformed to know and love God through the union of our minds with the Triune God."[49]

Preaching Theology

The preaching life for Thomas, therefore, is a theological life; it is the fruit of contemplation engendered by prayerful study of Holy Scripture, infused by divine grace and shaped by the virtues of faith, hope, and love. Nurtured to maturity by the gifts of the Holy Spirit, it is the imitation of Christ and the Way of friendship, communion with God.[50] Based on his reading of the Gospel accounts of Christ as exemplar, Thomas viewed the Dominicans as a guild of preachers whose vocation was to follow Jesus, engaging the world in the service of others — practical goodness — while nourishing this activity with prayerful contemplation:[51]

48. On the importance of *habitus*, see Romanus Cessario, O.P., *The Moral Virtues and Theological Ethics* (Notre Dame: University of Notre Dame Press, 1991), pp. 34-44.

49. Williams, "Mystical Theology Redux: The Pattern of Aquinas' *Summa Theologiae*," *Modern Theology* 13, no. 1 (1997): 69. See also Williams, *The Ground of Union: Deification in Aquinas and Palamas* (Oxford: Oxford University Press, 1999). In addition, see the excellent essay by Gilles Mongeau, S.J., "Aquinas' Spiritual Pedagogy," *Nova et Vetera* 2, no. 1 (2004): 91-114; and the discussion of divine friendship in Paul J. Wadell, C.P., *The Primacy of Love: An Introduction to the Ethics of Thomas Aquinas* (Mahwah, N.J.: Paulist Press, 1992), pp. 63-78.

50. Romanus Cessario, O.P., *Christian Faith and the Theological Life* (Washington, D.C.: Catholic University Press, 1996), pp. 1-12, 103-24.

51. See the excellent essays in *Christ among the Medieval Dominicans: Presentations of Christ in the Texts and Images of the Order of Preachers*, ed. Kent Emery Jr. and Joseph P. Wawrykow (Notre Dame: University of Notre Dame Press, 1998); Healy, *Thomas Aquinas: Theologian of the Christian Life*, pp. 28-32.

The contemplative life is better than the active life that solely concerns itself with bodily necessities; but the active life that consists in passing on to others through preaching and teaching truths that have been contemplated is more perfect than the solely contemplative life, for it presupposes a plentitude of contemplation. That is why Christ chose a life of this type. (*ST* 2/2.188.6; cf. 3.40.1-2)

A good example of Thomas's work as a homiletic theologian is the sermons, or collations, that Thomas preached in 1273 before large popular audiences in Naples. The sermons are catechetical in nature, covering the Apostles' Creed, *Credo*; the Lord's Prayer, *Pater*; and the Ten Commandments, *Decem precepta*.[52] Here Thomas demonstrates how doctrine, Scripture, and the Christian life are integrated within the wisdom of holy teaching in its pastoral expressions.

The truth communicated by the Creed, Lord's Prayer, and Decalogue correspond, respectively, to the theological virtues of faith, hope, and love, which unite us to God. These virtues, which are gifts of God, are discussed in Thomas's shorter *Compendium of Theology* and throughout the longer *Summa Theologiae*: the Creed, which is the summary of Scripture (the teaching on the virtue of faith — *ST* 2/2.1.1, 8-9); the Lord's Prayer, which expresses the desires that impel us toward salvation's end, that is, beatitude or happiness (the teaching on the virtue of hope — *ST* 2/2.17-20, 83); and the Decalogue, which is the Evangelical Law or the activity of the Spirit through the virtues (the teaching on charity, love of God, and love of neighbor — *ST* 1/2.100-102, 2/2.22-28).[53]

Thomas O'Meara comments that in Thomas's preaching, "there is a clarity and a directness, an attention to the theological."[54] Moreover, the scope of his explication of the Creed, the Lord's Prayer, and the Deca-

---

52. I am using *The Catechetical Instructions of St. Thomas Aquinas*, ed. and trans. Rev. Joseph B. Collins (Manila: Sinag-Tala Publishers, 1939); hereafter cited parenthetically according to particular sermon. See also Torrell, *Saint Thomas Aquinas*, 1:70-74; 2:322-40.

53. Cessario, *Christian Faith and the Theological Life*, pp. 1-9; see Cessario's description of preaching and the virtues, pp. 149-58. See also Cessario, *The Moral Virtues and Theological Ethics*, pp. 94-95.

54. O'Meara, *Thomas Aquinas: Theologian*, p. 39. In *Albert and Thomas*, Tugwell writes, "In his preaching, he appears to have cultivated a simple style without rhetorical flourishes. . . . His aim was to provide lucid, straightforward instruction" (p. 259). Presumably, Thomas had no interest in the pious stories and extravagant *exempla* utilized by popular preachers.

logue correspond to the spiritual senses of Scripture: what to believe, what to hope for, and what to love. These enabled Christians to follow Christ through adherence to the Triune God in the liturgical and sacramental life of the church.[55] The introductory sermon from each series of sermons, discussed below, suggests the scope of what follows in the remainder of Thomas's exposition.

The Apostles' Creed   The series on the Creed begins with the question "What is faith?" According to Thomas, faith is the first thing necessary for every Christian, and it brings about four good effects. The first is that through faith the soul is united to God, a union akin to marriage (*Credo*, 1). This effect is integral to the sacrament of baptism, which, when conducted with faith, brings salvation. The second effect of faith is that eternal life has already begun in the believer; for eternal life is nothing else than knowing God, which begins here and now through faith (*Credo*, 2).

The third effect of faith is the right direction it gives to our present life, which depends on what is taught by faith to be lived well. Thomas teaches that without faith in Christ, not even philosophers may know God through their own powers, nor the means necessary for salvation, but since Christ's coming, ordinary people have known him through the gift of faith (*Credo*, 3). The fourth effect of faith is that we are able to overcome temptation through belief in a better life to come, to despise the riches of this world and stand against its adversity. Thomas concludes that everything the Saints believed and handed down concerning the faith of Christ is signed with the seal of God. "And we need go no further. We are more certain, therefore, in believing the things of faith than those things that can be seen, because God's knowledge never deceives us, but the visible sense of man is often in error" (*Credo*, 4-5).

The Lord's Prayer   Thomas ascribes to the Lord's Prayer a chief place, since it displays five excellent qualities required of all Christian prayer: confidence, suitability, order, devotion, and humility (*Pater*, 157). First, prayer must be confident and not wanting in faith. To have confidence in

---

55. See the discussions of Thomas's interpretation of Scripture in Healy, *Thomas Aquinas: Theologian of the Christian Life*, pp. 41-47. See also Eugene F. Rogers Jr., *Thomas Aquinas and Karl Barth: Sacred Doctrine and the Natural Knowledge of God* (Notre Dame: University of Notre Dame Press, 1999), pp. 56-59.

the trustworthiness of the Lord's Prayer is most reasonable, since it was formed by Christ, our Advocate and most wise Petitioner. Moreover, this prayer is worthy of our confidence because of Christ, the One who taught us to pray, and who hears our prayers with his Father.

But prayer must also be suitable, asking what is right and fitting from God. Here Christ is our Teacher, who teaches us what we ought to pray. Moreover, prayer must also be ordered in such a way that our desires are rightly ordered, since prayer is an expression of desire. It is best, however, that in praying we desire spiritual rather than bodily things, the Kingdom of God and his justice.

According to Thomas, prayer must also be devout; a rich treasure of piety makes the sacrifice of prayer acceptable to God. It is important that prayer be brief, as the Lord's Prayer is; devotion can grow cold due to an excess of words. Most important, however, is that devotion in prayer arises from charity, from love of God and neighbor. Such charity is cultivated by praying to God as Father, by petitioning for the gift of forgiveness that produces the love of neighbor (*Pater*, 159).

Thomas adds that prayer must be humble, since the petitions of the meek are pleasing to God. True humility does not presume upon its own strength, but with the aid of divine strength expects all that is asked for. Thus, three effects characterize true prayer. First, prayer protects one from evil, from the fear of future sin, from trials and sadness of soul. Second, prayer that is efficacious for obtaining what one desires creates perseverance: "We always ought to pray and not to faint." Third and of utmost importance is that the profitability of prayer is that it makes us friends with God: "Let my prayer be directed as incense in thy sight" (*Pater*, 160).

The Ten Commandments   Thomas begins his sermons on the Ten Commandments with Christ, the Evangelical Law: "The entire law of Christ depends upon charity. And charity depends on two precepts, one concerns loving God and the other concerns loving our neighbor." Reading the Decalogue in a manner similar to that of Bonaventure, Thomas interprets the first three commandments as referring to the love of God and the latter seven commandments as related to love of neighbor, with both forms of love being centered on Jesus Christ (*Decem precepta*, 79). Several examples follow to demonstrate how the first commandment is most often violated: through the worship of demons, heavenly bodies,

84

the lower elements, and the many things of earth. Thomas offers a counter to these effects by listing five reasons why Christians ought always to worship the one true God: God's dignity and God's bounty toward humanity, the importance of human fidelity to God, the need for resistance against the devil, and most important, the promise of eternal reward: the glory of Angels (*Decem precepta*, 81).

Thomas's sermons on the Creed, the Lord's Prayer, and the Decalogue exemplify the practice of contemplation that overflows in the gift of Christian speech: holy teaching. Articulating a "knowing how" of entering into union with God by the means of divine grace, the theological virtues of faith, hope, and charity, Thomas's aim was to effect that which he spoke, drawing his listeners into the drama of creation and redemption, participating in the life of God as traced through the order and movement of the *Summa*:

> First, as regards the intellect, man receives certain supernatural principles, which are held by means of a Divine light; these are the articles of faith, about which is faith. — Secondly, the will is directed to this end, both as to the movement of intention, which tends to that end as something attainable, — and this pertains to hope, and as to a certain spiritual union, whereby the will is, so to speak, transformed into that end, and this belongs to charity. (*ST*, 1/2.62.3)

CHAPTER 4

Late Medieval Voices
in the Story of Sacred Rhetoric

The late medieval period was characterized by numerous expressions of spiritual hunger and desire for church renewal and reform. A driving force that provided much of the impetus for both intellectual and spiritual yearning was a return to the sources of Scripture, the Fathers, and the classical wisdom of antiquity. Of particular significance was the attention given to the grammatical and rhetorical study of Scripture to discover fresh understandings for its pastoral use in preaching and teaching.

Perhaps the most important figure in this pedagogical task of looking back in order to look forward was the Christian humanist Erasmus of Rotterdam. Through his teaching and writing in England and on the Continent, Erasmus provided pastors with both theological wisdom and practical instruction for their vocation, particularly the preaching of the Word of God. Although Erasmus, who was an Augustinian monk, did not preach, his work was highly influential among both Catholic and Protestant preachers.

A contemporary of Erasmus, Hugh Latimer, was arguably the most influential preacher in sixteenth-century England during the initial stirrings of reform. His ministry of the Word displays a clear Erasmian quality of "reformation through practice."

Erasmus of Rotterdam: Exemplar of Biblical Humanism

Historical Context

"Intellectual changes in Tudor England during the early sixteenth century stirred an increasing desire for biblically inspired personal regeneration and social reform."[1] Educational improvements and innovations at Cambridge University in the form of Christian humanism — most notably a return to the New Testament, the Church Fathers, and classical learning — stimulated a quantum leap in the importance of Scripture and its use in preaching for the renovation of the late medieval church.

The impact of John Fisher, as chancellor of Cambridge, and Erasmus, as visiting scholar, was instrumental in shaping a generation of preachers, prelates, and scholars who shared a common faith that would eventually divide them.[2] Prior to the existence of two distinct churches in England — Protestant and Catholic — Fisher and Erasmus worked to cultivate an intellectual and spiritual environment that created common ground for thinkers of diverse persuasions, thereby cultivating the rich soil in which significant English reformers and ideas of reform were able to flourish.

Continuing a trend that began in the fifteenth century, John Fisher (d. 1535), who was chancellor of Cambridge from 1504 to 1534, made an immense contribution to the development of the University into a center for traditional Christian scholarship and humanist learning, and especially devoted to cultivating a strong preaching ministry for the reform of

---

1. Horton Davies, *Worship and Theology in England: From Cranmer to Hooker, 1534-1603* (Princeton: Princeton University Press, 1970), vol. 2, pp. 227-54; Richard Rex, *Henry VIII and the English Reformation* (New York: Oxford University Press, 1993), pp. 76-78, 124-26; Lucy E. C. Wooding, *Rethinking Catholicism in Reformation England* (Oxford: Oxford University Press, 2000), pp. 16-48; Susan R. Wabuda, *Preaching during the English Reformation* (Cambridge: Cambridge University Press, 2003), pp. 117-19.

2. A. G. Dickens and Whitney R. D. Jones suggest that during the later 1510s the *Novum Instrumentum* of Erasmus rather than Luther would have commanded attention at the White Horse Inn. See Dickens and Jones, *Erasmus the Reformer* (London: Reed Books, 1995), p. 206; J. K. McConica, *English Humanists and Reformation Politics under Henry VIII and Edward VI* (Oxford: Clarendon Press, 1965), pp. 13-43, 76-105. For comments on notable graduates of late medieval Cambridge, see H. C. Porter, *Reformation and Reaction in Tudor Cambridge* (Cambridge: Cambridge University Press, 1991), pp. 3-20, 41-73; Richard Rex, *The Theology of John Fisher* (Cambridge: Cambridge University Press, 1991), pp. 12-30.

the church.[3] While he viewed traditional scholastic training in the arts as indispensable to the study of theology, Fisher also acknowledged the benefits of the "New Learning," the study of classical literature, languages, and rhetoric recovered by humanists for effective written and spoken communication. The preaching of the word of God, however, was the primary objective toward which all other intellectual and educational concerns were subordinated.[4]

To this end, Fisher was not content to rely on the past, but with an eye toward the future continued to expand the University's academic resources by attracting foreign scholars. The most important of these was Erasmus (d. 1536), who, during his longest visit at Cambridge, from 1511 to 1514, resided at Queen's College, teaching Greek and theology.[5]

Erasmus, Practitioner of Piety

During the past thirty years there has been a shift away from certain traditional interpretations of Erasmus, a bias shared by both Protestants and Catholics that has viewed him as a skeptic, indifferent or hostile to doctrine, a rationalist, and a precursor of enlightenment.[6] Recent interpreters,

3. Rex, *The Theology of John Fisher*, pp. 30-50; Brendan Bradshaw, "Bishop John Fisher, 1469-1535: The Man and His Work," in *Humanism, Reform, and the Reformation: The Career of Bishop John Fisher*, ed. Brendan Bradshaw and Eamon Duffy (Cambridge: Cambridge University Press, 1989), pp. 1-24; Wabuda, *Preaching during the English Reformation*, pp. 64-106.

4. Malcolm Underwood, "John Fisher and the Promotion of Learning," in *Humanism, Reform, and the Reformation*, ed. Bradshaw and Duffy, pp. 25-46; Rex, *The Theology of John Fisher*, pp. 50-64.

5. H. C. Porter and D. F. S. Thomson, *Erasmus and Cambridge* (Toronto: University of Toronto Press, 1963), pp. 25-92.

6. For discussion of shifts in interpretations of Erasmus, see Hilmar M. Pabel, *Conversing with God: Prayer in Erasmus' Pastoral Writings* (Toronto: University of Toronto Press, 1997), pp. 1-10; Pabel, "Promoting the Business of the Gospel: Erasmus' Contribution to Pastoral Ministry," *Erasmus of Rotterdam Society Yearbook* 15 (1995): 53-70; Manfred Hoffman, *Rhetoric and Theology: The Hermeneutic of Erasmus* (Toronto: University of Toronto Press, 1994), pp. 15-26; Hoffman, "Erasmus on Church and Ministry," in *Erasmus of Rotterdam Society Yearbook* 6 (1986): 1-30; John O'Malley, "Introduction," in *Collected Works of Erasmus*, vol. 66: *Spiritualia: Enchiridion, De Contemptu Mundi, De Vidua Christiana*, ed. John O'Malley (Toronto: University of Toronto Press, 1988), pp. ix-xxx; Cornelius Augustijn, *Erasmus: His Life, Works, and Influence*, trans. J. C. Grayson (Toronto: University of Toronto Press, 1986), pp. 185-200; Leon-E. Halkin, *Erasmus: A Critical Biography*, trans. John Tonkin (Oxford: Blackwell, 1987), pp. 289-96.

however, have viewed the main purpose of Erasmus's religious work as the practice of piety *(pietas)*. While Erasmus was not interested in writing theological books in the mode of scholastic discourse, he wanted to rouse his contemporaries from their spiritual slumbers, to awaken them into a revitalized Christian way of life and spirit devoted to loving God and neighbor through loving obedience to Christ and his "philosophy" *(philosophia)*.[7]

Although Erasmus was not primarily a preacher, his evangelical humanism articulated the intellectual and moral virtues that Fisher desired to impart in the formation of learned and devout preachers, thereby reuniting the activities of theology, ministry, and piety within the philosophy of Christ: sacred rhetoric derived from the holy pages of Scripture. Moreover, Erasmus's piety was corrective and reforming, in large part an alternative to much that was around him. His goal was to use the past as an instrument to correct, not confirm, the present.[8] As Erasmus communicated to Pope Leo X, "To restore great things is sometimes not only harder but a nobler task than to have introduced them."[9]

Significantly, Erasmus occupied a moderate position that cultivated both a Catholic sense for the traditional development of doctrine and a Protestant critique of tradition on the basis of the once-and-for-all evangelical standard established by the Gospel.[10] Because he hoped to provide both laity and clergy with a model of clear, simple, scriptural faith, he viewed patristic piety and wisdom as better and more fruitful than the arid, complex, and proud disputations of late medieval schoolmen that separated theology from the social practices of the church and led to what he perceived as malpractice in preaching and pastoral ministry.[11]

Writing to Jan Schlecta in November 1519, Erasmus offered a clear précis of this vision for his fellow priest:

7. Pabel, *Conversing with God*, pp. 4-5.

8. O'Malley, "Introduction," in *Collected Works of Erasmus*, vol. 66, p. xvii.

9. *Collected Works of Erasmus*, vol. 3: *Letters 298-445: 1514-1516*, trans. R. A. B. Mynors and D. F. S. Thomson (Toronto: University of Toronto Press, 1976), pp. 221-22.

10. Hoffman, *Rhetoric and Theology*, p. 268. See also the excellent discussion in Wabuda, *Preaching during the English Reformation*, pp. 64-80; John O'Malley, "Form, Content, and Influence of Works about Preaching before Trent: The Franciscan Contribution," in *Religious Culture in the Sixteenth Century: Preaching, Rhetoric, Spirituality, and Reform* (Burlington, Vt.: Ashgate Publishers, 1993).

11. Eugene F. Rice Jr., *Saint Jerome and the Renaissance* (Baltimore: Johns Hopkins University Press, 1985), p. 93.

Besides which the whole of Christian philosophy lies in this, our understanding that all our hope is placed in God, who freely gives us all things through Jesus his Son, that we were redeemed by his death and engrafted through baptism with his body, that we might be dead to the desires of this world and live by his teaching and example, not merely harbouring no evil by deserving well of all men; so that, if adversity befall, we may bear it bravely in hope of the future reward which beyond question awaits all good men at Christ's coming, and that we may ever advance from one virtue to another, yet in such a way that we claim nothing for ourselves, but ascribe any good we do to God.[12]

Erasmus viewed himself as a steward of Christ's philosophy in the cure of souls; his writings enabled him to speak through priests to minister to Christians, applying to their lives and for their benefit the teaching and wisdom of Scripture.[13] As Marjorie O'Rourke Boyle comments, "If Erasmus had wished, he could have mounted the pulpits of Europe. He was no preacher, however, but a teacher of teachers. The printing press could straddle the Continent more effectively than any sermon, and it served him well."[14] In spreading *docta pietas* — learned piety — through the written word, Erasmus committed himself to the business of the Gospel, which he hoped would bear fruit in godly wisdom and virtue. Thus the aim of conversion and transformation was constitutive of all he wrote, "the seamless robe of his *pietas*."[15]

Novum Instrumentum

In March 1516 Erasmus published the long-awaited *Novum Instrumentum*, directing considerable attention to the subject of Scripture and its impor-

12. *Collected Works of Erasmus*, vol. 7: *Letters 993-1121: 1519-1520*, trans. R. A. B. Mynors, ed. Peter G. Beitenholz (Toronto: University of Toronto Press, 1987), pp. 126-27. See the excellent discussion of Erasmus's use of biblical scholarship for training clergy and laity to distinguish between faithful and unfaithful pastoral practice in Jane E. Philips, "The Gospel, the Clergy, and the Laity in Erasmus' 'Paraphrase on the Gospel of John,'" *Erasmus of Rotterdam Society Yearbook* 10 (1990): 85-100.

13. Pabel, *Conversing with God*, p. 9.

14. O'Rourke Boyle, *Erasmus on Language and Method in Theology* (Toronto: University of Toronto Press, 1977), p. 69.

15. O'Malley, "Introduction," in *Collected Works of Erasmus*, vol. 66, p. xxx.

tance for the church.[16] It consisted of a dedication, followed by preliminary matters: the *Paraclesis, Methodus,* and *Apologia,* respectively a persuasive appeal to read the New Testament, guides for its use, and a defense of the undertaking. The Greek text was provided with a Latin translation by Erasmus himself. Finally came the *Annotations,* Erasmus's notes on the text, which take up almost as much space as the Latin and Greek texts put together. The introductory material pleads for a theology that would start from the words and concepts appearing in Scripture, promoting the normalization of biblical language as an instrument for bridging the gap between theology and pastoral practice. As he once noted, "I see how simple people, who hang open-mouthed on the lips of the preacher, yearn for food for the soul, eager to learn how they can go home better people."[17]

In the introductory letter to the general reader, Erasmus explains how he produced the work, describing it as "the humblest service in pious devotion," and "a work of piety, a Christian work." Its purpose is to render Scripture more eloquent, lucid, and faithful to the apostolic discourse, thereby showing forth Christ and finding more followers for his sacred philosophy. This is repeated in the dedicatory letter to Pope Leo X, whom Erasmus addressed as "a second Esdras, a re-builder of the Christian religion." He offered the pope the *Novum Instrumentum* as a gift for the daily advancement of the Christian life.[18]

Erasmus chose the title *Instrumentum,* which may mean "organ," "instrument," or "means of teaching and writing."[19] His purified text of the New Testament is an instrument for the philosophy of Christ, the living Word spoken by the Father and revealed in Scripture. A striking and controversial expression of its rhetorical purpose appeared in the 1519 edition, which rendered the translation of John 1:1, "In the beginning was the Word," as *sermo* rather than *verbum,* meaning not simply words uttered singly but discourse that is concentrated, eloquent, and meaningful. By this Erasmus means that Christ is the sermon of God, divine wisdom and eloquence incarnate who, in the writings of the evangelists and apostles, "still lives and breathes for us and acts and speaks with more immediate

16. For a good discussion, see Erika Rummel, *The Humanist-Scholastic Debate in the Renaissance and Reformation* (Cambridge: Harvard University Press, 1998), pp. 96-125.

17. Cited in Augustijn, *Erasmus,* p. 103.

18. *Collected Works of Erasmus,* vol. 3, pp. 204, 222.

19. R. J. Schoeck, *Erasmus of Europe: The Making of a Humanist: 1500-1536* (Edinburgh: Edinburgh University Press, 1992), p. 190.

efficacy than any other way." The written word of Scripture is the incarnation of divinity, and the spirit of this word possesses the power of revelation. Replete with the authority of God, the sacred text is alive with the presence of Christ as the transcendent and transforming Word who speaks through human speech.[20]

Erasmus, therefore, viewed his biblical scholarship as an instrument for communicating the enlivening power of Christ to readers. This purpose was embodied in the *Paraclesis,* the classic statement of his biblical humanism.[21] Written in the form of a doxological hymn that praises the philosophy of Christ, the *Paraclesis,* or word of exhortation, appeals to Christians to read with a desire that they be translated into the message of the New Testament.[22] Although Erasmus wrote his short "trumpet blast" to address a general readership, its startling force was felt particularly by preachers, generating an immediate response that anticipated its eventual popularity among Protestants, who were drawn to its strong focus on the eloquent speech of Christ through the medium of Scripture.[23]

Erasmus's striking claim is that Scripture, if used appropriately, speaks with sufficient persuasiveness to accomplish its spiritual purpose: to render the living mind and image of Christ and to draw listeners into the transforming power and mystical union of divine love: charity seeking charity.[24] This requires rhetoric appropriate to its sacred subject, even if less ornate than sophistry, which aims to stimulate pleasure and delight. In contrast to

---

20. O'Rourke Boyle, *Erasmus on Language and Method in Theology,* pp. 1-57; Hoffman, *Rhetoric and Theology,* pp. 81-93; Stephen H. Webb, *The Divine Voice: Christian Proclamation and the Theology of Sound* (Grand Rapids: Brazos Press, 2004), pp. 130-34; Deborah Shuger, *Sacred Rhetoric* (Princeton: Princeton University Press, 1988).

21. *Paraclesis, id est, Adhortatio ad Christianae Philosphiae Studium,* trans. John Olin, in *Christian Humanism and the Reformation: Selected Writings of Erasmus,* ed. John Olin (New York: Fordham University Press, 1987), pp. 97-108; hereafter cited parenthetically in the text as *Paraclesis.*

22. Augustijn, *Erasmus,* pp. 78-79. O'Malley, "Introduction," in *Collected Works of Erasmus,* vol. 66, p. xxvi.

23. Dickens and Jones, *Erasmus the Reformer,* p. 198. See the assessment of Margaret Mann Phillips in *Erasmus and the Northern Renaissance* (Woodbridge, 1981): "Almost all the ideas expressed in the *Paraclesis* were in accordance with those expressed by Luther" (p. 85).

24. According to Marjorie O'Rourke Boyle, "Rhetoric seeks an act of the will, assent, and secures its end in religious conversion." See "Rhetorical Theology: Charity Seeking Charity," in *Rhetorical Invention and Religious Inquiry: New Perspectives,* ed. Walter Jost and Wendy Olmstead (New Haven and London: Yale University Press, 2000), p. 90.

the fleeting futility of classical oratory, the eloquence of Scripture renders the wisdom of Christ, which "not only captivates the ear, but which leaves a lasting sting in the minds of its hearers, which grips, which transforms, which sends away a far different listener than it received." Unhindered by human syllogisms and exclamations, Scripture, through the Spirit's power, inflames the heart to sing Christ's praise (*Paraclesis*, 98). The *Paraclesis* therefore extended a compelling invitation to Christians to develop new capacities of reading and speaking Scripture in a life-changing manner.

According to Erasmus, only the new and wonderful philosophy of Christ is worthy of wholehearted devotion and pursuit. Offering a simpler and more satisfying form of life than all human philosophies, this wisdom is acquired through intimate attachment to its Author and Prince, Christ, the teacher who came forth from heaven. Erasmus thus sings the praise of Christ, who alone can teach certain doctrine, since it is eternal wisdom; Christ alone, the sole author of human salvation, taught what pertains to salvation; Christ alone vouches for whatever he taught and is able to grant whatsoever he has promised (*Paraclesis*, 99).

Why is Christ's philosophy unique? Erasmus declares, "To teach this wisdom God became man; He who was in the heart of the Father descended to earth, rendering foolish the entire wisdom of the world." Not even the wisdom of philosophy can yield knowledge of Christ; only a pious, open mind and simple faith will do. "The journey is simple, and is ready for anyone." Advancement in the Way is granted to the docile and humble, those whom Christ inspires as a good teacher by communicating the grammar of piety to eager young minds (*Paraclesis*, 100).

According to Erasmus, Christ accommodates his wisdom to all who love him; his embrace includes the highest to the lowest, regardless of one's position in life. Christ and his wisdom are more readily available than the sun; while the proud are excluded from his reach, even the humble and lowly share in his riches, the Gospels and the Epistles: "The farmer sings some portion of them at his plow, the weaver hums some parts of them to the movement of his shuttle, the traveler lightens the weariness of the journey with stories of this kind" (*Paraclesis*, 101).[25]

---

25. Lucy Wooding observes, "So the humanist effort was not restricted to scholarly pursuits and the world of intellectual elites. Its clear objective was the education and salvation of simple folk, and this aim was to unleash a flood of vernacular literature." See *Rethinking Catholicism in Reformation England*, p. 22.

The language of Scripture, therefore, is the medium by which Christian conversation and life are renewed (*Paraclesis*, 101). This possibility exists because the divine *sermo* came into the world through the word of Christ, who is the ultimate expression of the divine nature and power. Moreover, when Christ's word is received and translated into life, a person begins to speak a living language, simply and from the heart; the spirit of Christ inspires human speech. As Manfred Hoffman observes, "Language plays a pivotal role in Erasmus' thinking. . . . The truth of both the sensible and intelligible world is so deeply embedded in the word that there is no other way to comprehend it than by reading and hearing, and no other way to communicate it than by writing and speaking."[26]

The *Paraclesis* was heard throughout Christendom as a persuasive call to take up the practice of reading and speaking Scripture as a means of transformation to a holy life. Erasmus exulted in the generative power of Christ's wisdom, the rebirth of humanity and its restoration by God to its original goodness. Because this wisdom, the Divine Word, has been perfectly proclaimed in the Gospels and the Epistles, it is inscribed with power to effect what its Author has spoken. Everything that is required has been provided for those who desire to learn of Christ: a teacher and model to imitate, divine happiness and satisfaction for the mind, healing for troubled souls, passion and strength for the journey: "Let us, therefore, with our whole heart covet this literature, let us embrace it, at length let us die in its embrace, let us be transformed in it, since indeed studies are transmuted into morals" (*Paraclesis*, 102). Erasmus urged Christians to redirect their vision to the words and images of Scripture, to "the living image of His [Christ's] holy mind and the speaking, healing, dying, rising Christ Himself . . . so fully present that you would see less if you gazed upon Him with your very eyes" (*Paraclesis*, 102-3).[27]

---

26. Hoffman, *Rhetoric and Theology*, p. 61; Richard J. Schoeck, *Erasmus Grandescens* (Nieuwkoop: De Graaf, 1988), pp. 83-84; Rex, *The Theology of John Fisher*, pp. 60-61; O'Rourke Boyle, *Erasmus on Language and Method in Theology*, pp. 100-101.

27. For a discussion of Erasmus's critique of late medieval piety and its reliance on images, see Carlos M. N. Eire, *War against the Idols: The Reformation of Worship from Erasmus to Calvin* (Cambridge: Cambridge University Press, 1996), pp. 36-45. Eire observes, "Erasmus, in the first place, considered religious images as powerless. . . . The Christian ought to revere the portrait of God's mind that the skill of the Holy Spirit has portrayed in the writing of the Gospels" (p. 39). On Erasmus's view of history and human responsibility for the

Although written for a general audience, the *Paraclesis* produced significant implications for preachers, since it demonstrated a lively faith in the real presence of Christ rendered by the scriptural text, the divine *sermo* of the Father spoken in the persuasive power of the Spirit, uniting Scripture, rhetoric, and reform. For Erasmus, Christ is the living word of God, the image of God's mind, and as such he is the supreme preacher endowed with the utmost power of persuasion. In Christ's school of preaching, therefore, reading and listening precede speaking, wisdom comes before style, and truth before expression. As Erasmus asserts, "The special goal of theologians is to expound scripture wisely; to render its doctrine according to faith, not frivolous questions; to discourse about piety gravely and efficaciously, to wring out tears, to inflame spirits to heavenly things."[28]

Moreover, the better and clearer the theology, when particularly taught by Christ, the more persuasively the human heart may bring forth wisdom of sacred rhetoric in human speech.[29] Susan Wabuda concludes that for Erasmus, "The person of the preacher was the pivot, in the sacredness of the moment, the mouthpiece of the wisdom of God, infused with the spirit of Christ, who dwelt in his heart."[30] One who presumes to speak God's word must be so consumed and transformed by whom and what one knows that one becomes a living sermon, an instrument of the word of Christ, who "preaches, teaches, inculcates, exhorts, incites, and encourages" (*Paraclesis*, 102).[31]

Paraphrases on the New Testament

The wisdom of the *Novum Instrumentum* was supplemented by the publication of the *Paraphrases on the New Testament* (1517-24), providing preachers

---

past, see Istvan Bejczy, *Erasmus and the Middle Ages: The Historical Consciousness of a Christian Humanist* (Leiden: Brill, 2001), pp. 182-90.

28. Cited in O'Rourke Boyle, "Rhetorical Theology," p. 88.

29. See Shuger's *Sacred Rhetoric* for a discussion of the emphasis placed by Renaissance rhetorics on the passion of the preacher's heart and speech being inflamed by divine charity (pp. 221-40).

30. Wabuda, *Preaching during the English Reformation*, pp. 69, 65-69. See also the discussion in John O'Malley, "Erasmus and the History of Sacred Rhetoric," chapter 7 in *Religious Culture in the Sixteenth Century*.

31. Hoffman, "Erasmus on Church and Ministry," pp. 23-25. I am indebted to Hoffman's essay in formulating these two paragraphs.

with a continuous exposition of Scripture that rendered the philosophy of Christ in a clear and persuasive homiletic style.[32] Cardinal Campeggi wrote to Erasmus in 1519, "I seized every opportunity to acquire your image, which I found reflected . . . most recently in your sermon-paraphrase on the Pauline Epistles."[33] The sermon paraphrase, which was an instrument that allowed Erasmus to preach with pen and printing press, "says things differently without saying different things, especially in a subject which is not only difficult, but sacred, and very near the majesty of the Gospel."[34]

In these paraphrases Erasmus's goal was to render the genuine meaning of the biblical text, offering more than translation but less than commentary, communicating *by means of* the language of Scripture rather than *about* the language of Scripture. Erasmus hoped the reader would not be offended by the fact that he had changed the words of Holy Scripture in order to enable the voice of Paul or even of Christ to be heard. Thus the rhetorical purpose of the *Paraphrases* was to get the mind of Christ out of the pages of Scripture and into the minds of readers, since in spiritual regeneration Christ is the content, purpose, and final efficient cause.[35] When used in this manner, the words of Scripture and the words of the *Paraphrases* would serve a mediating function, respectively, between Christ and the church, Erasmus and his readers, preachers and their people.[36]

By accommodating himself to both the biblical text and the contemporary context, Erasmus presented himself as a model of pastoral discourse.[37] In the preaching of the Gospel, as in the writing of homiletic paraphrase on it, the spirit of Christ proceeds through the soul (or mind) of the preacher into the soul of the hearer or reader.[38] In the Paraphrase

---

32. Augustijn, *Erasmus*, pp. 99-102; Albert Rabil Jr., *Erasmus and the New Testament: The Mind of a Christian Humanist* (San Antonio: Trinity University Press, 1972), pp. 115-41.

33. *Collected Works of Erasmus*, vol. 7, p. 5.

34. *Collected Works of Erasmus*, vol. 5: *Letters 594-841: 1517-1518*, trans. R. A. B. Mynors and D. F. S. Thomson (Toronto: University of Toronto Press, 1979), p. 196.

35. J. J. Bateman, "From Soul to Soul: Persuasion in Erasmus' 'Paraphrases on the New Testament,'" *Erasmus in English* 15 (1987-88): 8.

36. *Collected Works of Erasmus*, vol. 42: *Paraphrases on Romans and Galatians*, trans. John B. Payne, Albert Rabil Jr., and Warren S. Smith Jr., ed. Robert D. Sider (Toronto: University of Toronto Press, 1984), pp. xiv-xviii. See also Albert Rabil Jr., "Erasmus's Paraphrases on the New Testament," in *Essays on the Works of Erasmus*, ed. Richard DeMolen (New Haven: Yale University Press, 1978), pp. 145-62.

37. *Collected Works of Erasmus*, vol. 42, pp. x-xii; Bateman, "From Soul to Soul," pp. 7-16.

38. Bateman, "From Soul to Soul," pp. 13-14.

on 1 Peter 4, Erasmus describes how this spiritual transformation enables the word of Christ to be spoken and heard:

> If it falls to a person's lot to receive sacred doctrine or the gift of a learned tongue, he is not to use it for personal gain or pride or empty glory but for the salvation of his neighbor and the glory of Christ, and his audience should perceive that the words they hear are from God, not from men, and that the one who speaks to them is but an instrument of the divine voice.[39]

Through his sermon paraphrases, Erasmus identified himself with pastors, instructing and encouraging them for the highest calling and function: to spread the teaching of the Gospel. His biblical scholarship paved the way for others to prove what Scripture could actually achieve through the acquisition of new intellectual habits and dispositions shaped by learned piety and embodied in the practice of pastoral ministry.[40] As Manfred Hoffman notes, "Erasmus wished for the church's external means of grace to operate according to their spiritual purpose. This pertains particularly to the ministry of proclaiming God's word incarnate in Christ and the Scripture."[41]

Preaching persuasively with his pen, Erasmus issued an enthusiastic call for preachers to take up the evangelistic task of making Christians by means of the message and spirit of Christ in Scripture by reuniting doctrine, rhetoric, and reform.[42] Just as Christ is the image and embodiment of God's Son, the Bible is the "inscripturation" of Christ's image and Spirit, capable of regenerating faith, spiritual vitality, and moral commitment by means of human speech.[43] By emphasizing the need for pastors

---

39. *Collected Works of Erasmus*, vol. 44: *Paraphrases on the Epistles to Timothy, Titus, and Philemon; The Epistles to Peter and Jude; The Epistle of James; The Epistles of John; The Epistle to the Hebrews*, trans. John J. Bateman, ed. Robert D. Sider (Toronto: University of Toronto Press, 1993), p. 103.

40. On Erasmus's rhetorical reading of Scripture, see Shuger, *Sacred Rhetoric*, pp. 243-49.

41. Hoffman, "Erasmus on Church and Ministry," p. 27.

42. Shuger, *Sacred Rhetoric*, pp. 200-211; Peter Matheson, *The Imaginative World of the Reformation* (Edinburgh: T&T Clark, 2000), pp. 1-24, 119-40; O'Malley, "Introduction," in *Collected Works of Erasmus*, vol. 66, pp. xxv-xxx.

43. Eire, *War against the Idols*, pp. 38-41; O'Rourke Boyle, *Erasmus on Language and Method in Theology*, p. 83; Matheson, *The Imaginative World of the Reformation*, pp. 125-26.

to learn, absorb, and rely upon the wisdom and persuasiveness of Scripture, Erasmus developed a rhetorical theology — *theologica rhetorica*. The business of preaching is simply Christ, the eloquent "sermon" of God who communicates himself through the learned piety and speech of pastors who are his "living sermons."[44] Susan Wabuda writes,

> Erasmus unleashed a bold new vision of what the preacher should be: dedicated and humble yet imposing; the vessel of God, yet unafraid to wield the authority of the deity too, no matter what the personal cost, even if it led to martyrdom. The connection between priest and preacher was inseparable. . . . The simple spirituality and rigor that had been traditionally associated with the episcopate and mendicant orders Erasmus now extended throughout the entire priesthood.[45]

Hugh Latimer: Exemplar of English Evangelism

Historical Context

For listeners in Tudor England, a sermon by Hugh Latimer was a significant religious and social event.[46] During the Protestant reign of Edward VI (1547-1553), Latimer (d. 1555) was arguably the most popular and persuasive preacher in the realm, announcing the word of God in a fresh, vibrant way to promote renewal in the church and regeneration of the social order. His itinerant preaching ministry required him to address a variety of audiences, from the king's court to common country folk, and on occasion he spoke before large crowds at the outdoor pulpit adjacent to St. Paul's, London. From late 1550 until Edward's death in 1553, however, Latimer was the most notable among a company of preachers that

44. On Augustine's influence in the sixteenth century, see Shuger, *Sacred Rhetoric*, pp. 47-65; Peter Iver Kaufman, *Augustinian Piety and Catholic Reform: Augustine, Colet, and Erasmus* (Macon: Mercer University Press, 1982), pp. 111-28. On rhetorical theology, see O'Malley, "Introduction," in *Collected Works of Erasmus*, vol. 66, pp. xxviii-ix; Charles Trinkaus, *In Our Image and Likeness*, 2 vols. (Chicago: University of Chicago Press, 1970), 1: 126-28.

45. Wabuda, *Preaching during the English Reformation*, p. 70.

46. Hugh Latimer, *The Works*, 2 vols. ed. George Corrie, The Parker Society (Cambridge: Cambridge University Press, 1968); hereafter cited parenthetically in the text as *Works*.

ploughed the fields of the English countryside, sowing the seed of the Word to evangelize and edify popular audiences. Christopher Haigh describes these preachers, calling them "as remarkable a group of evangelists as can ever be seen."[47]

David Steinmetz has written of the reforming perspective and purpose of Latimer's generation, the first among sixteenth-century Protestants:

> What set the Protestant message off from the medieval tradition was not the uniqueness of its questions or the newness of its sources. What set it off was the angle of vision from which these traditional sources were read and evaluated. The Christian past was not so much rejected by the Protestant reformers as refashioned in the light of a different and competing vision of its development and continuing significance.[48]

For Tudor England, the refashioning of a Protestant church and polity was advanced through the implementation of Thomas Cranmer's liturgical reforms.[49] Thus, the significant role played by common worship in the formation of a sixteenth-century commonwealth provides the larger framework for understanding Latimer's popular sermons in

47. Haigh, *English Reformations: Religion, Politics, and Society under the Tudors* (Oxford: Oxford University Press, 1993), p. 189. For a good description of the Edwardians' commitment to preaching, see Haigh, *English Reformations*, pp. 189-202; Catherine Davies, *A Religion of the Word* (Manchester: Manchester University Press, 2002), pp. 87-93; Robert Whiting, *Local Responses to the English Reformation* (New York: St. Martin's Press, 2000), pp. 167-82; Christopher Marsh, *Popular Religion in Sixteenth-Century England* (New York: St. Martin's Press, 1999), pp. 32-42, 52-54, 119-22; Robert Whiting, *The Blind Devotion of the People: Popular Religion and the English Reformation* (Cambridge: Cambridge University Press, 1989), pp. 234-55; Nicholas Tyacke, "Introduction: Re-thinking the 'English Reformation,'" in *England's Long Reformation, 1500-1800*, ed. Nicholas Tyacke (London: Ashgate Publishers, 1998), pp. 4-7.

48. Steinmetz, "The Intellectual Appeal of the Reformation," *Theology Today* 57, no. 4 (2001): 460-61.

49. According to Judith Maltby, "There was probably no other single aspect of the Reformation in England which touched more directly and fundamentally the consciousness, or lack of it, of ordinary clergy and laity, than did the reform of rituals and liturgy." See her *Prayer Book and People in Elizabethan and Early Stuart England* (Cambridge: Cambridge University Press, 1998), p. 4. See also the conclusions drawn by Sharon Arnoult, "Spiritual and Sacred Publique Actions: The Book of Common Prayer and the Understanding of Worship in the Elizabethan and Jacobean Church of England," in *Religion and the English People, 1500-1640: New Voices, New Perspectives*, ed. Eric Josef Carlson, Sixteenth-Century Essays and Studies, vol. 45 (Kirksville, Mo.: Truman State University Press, 1998), pp. 25-48.

Lincolnshire. The *Royal Injunctions* promulgated in July 1547 required every parish church in England to have "the whole Bible, of the largest volume in Englishe," Erasmus's *Paraphrases on the Gospels and Acts*, and a collection of twelve official sermons, known as the *Book of Homilies*, for use in reading, Bible study, and, most importantly, parish preaching.[50]

Cranmer's concern in producing the homilies was to establish the nature of salvation as God's free gift of faith, while demonstrating to preachers and persons in the pew that this affirmation did not result in the collapse of morality, that good works still formed an essential part of the Christian life. Because the Bible was the chief source for the rhetoric of the homilies, their aim was to imitate the language of Scripture, and in particular its figures and examples, thus replacing religious images with the verbal image of the Word — *pictura* with *scriptura*. This biblically derived style rendered the sermons more forceful and vivid, and increased their clarity and immediacy while keeping their teaching grounded in the soil of Scripture. In this manner, the vision of a Christian realm set forth in the homilies offered fitting and persuasive models for preaching, unfolding a way of life in which listeners were called to acquire knowledge of Scripture and faith in Christ, which were expressed in good works through charity in accordance with God's commandments.[51]

Moreover, the distinctive marks of the sixteenth-century English Church, the *Ecclesia Anglicana*, included its recovery of the Bible in the vernacular as a living text addressed to English folk. By placing the prayer book, basic Christian texts, and liturgical events at the center of religious discourse, Cranmer sought to construct a renewed Church of England built upon a theology of the Word, believing that biblical speech, faithfully presented in its various forms, possessed the power to transform the world in which it is spoken, heard, and obeyed. Thus, the transformation of England into a Christian commonwealth was to be realized through participation in the grace of Christ and active love of neighbor, visible signs of citizenship in the Kingdom of God.[52] The theological sig-

---

50. John N. Wall, *Transformations of the Word: Spenser, Herbert, and Vaughn* (Athens: University of Georgia Press, 1988), pp. 11-15.

51. *"Certain Sermons and Homilies (1547)"* and *"A Homily Against Disobedience and Wilful Rebellion (1570),"* ed. Ronald B. Bond (Toronto: University of Toronto Press, 1987), p. 3; John N. Wall, "Godly and Fruitful Lessons," in *The Godly Kingdom of Tudor England: Great Books of the English Reformation*, ed. John E. Booty (Wilton, Conn.: Morehouse-Barlow, 1981), pp. 95-103.

52. Wall, *Transformations of the Word*, pp. 11-15.

nificance that Latimer attached to liturgical reform was affirmed in the preface to the 1549 *Book of Common Prayer*:

> There was never anything by the wit of man so well devised or so sure established, which in continuance of time hath not been corrupted, as among other things, it may plainly appear by the common prayers in the Church, commonly called Divine Service. The first and original ground whereof if a man would search out by the ancient Fathers; he shall find that the same was not ordained but of a good purpose and for a great advancement of godliness. For they so ordered the matter that the whole Bible (or the greatest part thereof) should be read over once every year; intending thereby that the clergy, and especially such as were ministers in the congregation, should be stirred up to godliness themselves, and be more able to exhort others by wholesome doctrine, and to confute them that were adversaries to the truth; and further that the people (by daily reading of Holy Scripture in the Church) might continually profit more and more in the knowledge of God and be more inflamed with the love of his true religion.[53]

John King comments on the significance of the new prayer book: "Gone forever was the supremacy of the medieval mass, which had been celebrated out of the sight of the people in a language they could not understand." This union of common prayer through common language promoted a communal dialogue between a speaking, summoning God and a listening, responding people; thus, biblically mediated colloquy replaced the medieval distinction between priest and people.[54] The 1552 *Act of Uni-*

---

53. *Documents of the English Reformation*, ed. Gerald Bray (Minneapolis: Augsburg Publishing House, 1994), p. 273. In *Thomas Cranmer: A Life* (London: Yale University Press, 1996), Diarmaid MacCulloch uses the term "reformed Catholic" to describe the position of Cranmer, which also could apply to Latimer: "For they [the reformers] sought to build up the Catholic Church on the same foundations of Bible, creeds, and the great councils of the early Church. . . . Cranmer was guiding the Church of England to a renewed Catholicity through thickets of wicked deceit which must be avoided at all costs: on the one hand, papistry, and on the other, Anabaptism, both equally 'sects' in his eyes" (p. 617). Note also Paul Avis's comment in *Anglicanism and the Christian Church* (Oxford: Oxford University Press, 1988): "Particular (i.e., national) churches are catholic when they profess and teach the faith and religion of Christ according to the scripture and apostolic doctrine" (p. 35).

54. King, *English Reformation Literature: The Tudor Origins of the Protestant Tradition* (Princeton: Princeton University Press, 1982), pp. 135-36.

formity, announcing the implementation of a revised *Book of Common Prayer,* refers to its "very godly order . . . to be used in the mother tongue within the Church of England . . . very comfortable to all good people desiring to live in Christian conversation . . . by common prayers, due using of the sacraments, and frequent preaching of the Word of God with the devotion of its hearers."[55]

Latimer, Master of Plain Preaching

Latimer was arguably the outstanding exemplar of the colloquial style among sixteenth-century English preachers.[56] His plain style of preaching, in imitation of the English of the Bible, was a form of speech that facilitated conversation with and conversion of the broadest possible audience — universal and catholic — thus granting his sermons a flavor that has prompted historians to categorize him as a "typically medieval preacher."[57] Indeed, Latimer's popularizing style, marked by its picturesque imagery, earthy diction, and figures of speech, enabled him to communicate through direct, concrete, unadorned, passionate language, displaying obvious continuities with the best of patristic and medieval preaching *ad populum.*[58] H. O. Taylor vividly describes Latimer's use of language:

> He drew his convictions from the Scriptures as spontaneously as he drew the illustrations of them from the world around him. His sermons reflected and absorbed the habits, the demands, the hardships,

55. *Documents of the English Reformation,* ed. Bray, p. 281.

56. J. W. Blench, *Preaching in England in the late Fifteenth and Sixteenth Centuries* (Oxford: Oxford University Press, 1964), pp. 142-53; Harold S. Darby, *Hugh Latimer: A Biography* (London: Epworth Press, 1953), pp. 201-55; Robert Demaus, *Hugh Latimer: A Biography* (Nashville: Abingdon Press, 1869), pp. 468-71; Charles Smyth, *The Art of Preaching in the Church of England: 747-1939* (London, 1940), p. 107.

57. Smyth, *The Art of Preaching in the Church of England,* p. 107. In volume 1 of *Worship and Theology in England,* Horton Davies comments, "Latimer was a people's preacher, not a preacher's preacher" (p. 248). See G. R. Owst's description of medieval popular preaching in his *Preaching in Medieval England* (Cambridge: Cambridge University Press, 1926), pp. 253-333.

58. See Shuger's comment in *Sacred Rhetoric:* "In England, the vernacular sacred rhetorics tend to carry on the medieval passionate plain style under Protestant auspices" (pp. 243-44).

the very implements and incidents of English life, all straight from the preacher to his audience. Here indeed was an English Gospeller whose thoughts and phrases seemed to echo Wyclif: "right prelating is busy labouring, and not lording" might have been Wyclif's or Latimer's.[59]

The issue of language and style in popular preaching was not only a social concern but also reflected theological and moral issues that were bound up with the reformation of church and society in England. The Reformers viewed the Bible as the book of the people, and through its regulated use they were to become a people of the book. A challenge facing preachers like Latimer, however, was that of being able to bridge the gap between "high and low," the capacity to open new lines of communication to include both learned piety and popular devotion. This required the discovery of plain, fitting speech to articulate Scripture's message for the enactment of lively faith, language sufficiently inviting for drawing diverse audiences, persuasive enough for overcoming indifference or resistance to revival. In the preface to the *Great Bible,* the first English-lanugage Bible authorized for public use, Cranmer wrote,

> Here may all manner of persons, men, women, young, old, learned, unlearned, rich, poor, priests, laymen, lords, ladies, officers, tenants, and mean men, virgins, wives, widows, lawyers, merchants, artificers, husbandmen, and all manner of persons, of what estate or condition soever they be, may in THIS BOOK learn all things, that they ought to believe, what they ought to do, and what they should not do, as well concerning Almighty God, as also concerning themselves, and all other.[60]

The humble style demonstrated by popular preachers such as Latimer was intended to reflect the *ethos* of Scripture and to make the message of the Word, its inward, spiritual truth, available to all without intimidating or repelling the unlearned. Thus in popular preaching, the lowly, earthy style incarnate in Christ and embodied in Scripture, which was favored by the Fathers — *sermo humilis* — was capable of overcoming barriers that might impede hearing, evoking a world of the divine accom-

---

59. Taylor, *Thought and Expression in the Sixteenth Century* (New York: Constable, 1959), p. 125.

60. *Documents of the English Reformation,* ed. Bray, pp. 238-39.

modating itself to the lowly in the plain, humble Word through preachers who exemplified its character.[61] Moreover, humility was the primary intellectual and moral virtue necessary for producing competent speaking, hearing, and enacting the message incarnate in Scripture, the embodiment or performance of the Bible, as prescribed by the *Book of Homilies*:

> Read it [Holy Scripture] humbly, with a meke and lowly harte, to thintent you maie glorifie God, and not your self, with the knowledge of it; and reade it not without daily praiying to God that he would direct your readying to good effecte; and take upon you to expounde it no further than you can plainly understande it. For, as St. Augustine saieth, the knowledge of Holy Scripture is a great, large, and high palace, but the door is verie lowe so that the high and arrogant man cannot runne in, but he must stoupe and humble hym self that shall entre into it.[62]

Latimer expressed this conviction at the beginning of a sermon he preached in Lincolnshire, asserting that both the preaching and the hearing of the Word are dependent upon the activity of the Triune God to evoke living faith. The Spirit enables the Word to accomplish its divine purpose, generating faith and obedience to the living God. He thus bid his audience to "call upon God in the name of Christ to give unto us the Holy Ghost — unto me, that I may speak the Word of God, and teach you to understand the same; that you may hear it fruitfully, to the edification of your souls; so that you may be edified through it, and your lives emended and reformed; and that his honour and glory may increase daily amongst us" (*Works*, I. 455-56).

Worship in the church of this period, therefore, did not seek to lift its participants to another, higher realm or world, a purpose the Reformers ascribed pejoratively to the medieval mass. Rather, the evangelicals' use of the Bible in common prayer and preaching sought to make of common places theaters of divine revelation, scenes of vivid, dramatic perfor-

61. Eric Auerbach, *Literary Language and Its Public in Late Antiquity and in the Middle Ages*, trans. Ralph Manheim (Princeton: Princeton University Press, 1993), pp. 39-47. See also the excellent discussion by Peter Auski, *Christian Plain Style: The Evolution of a Spiritual Ideal* (Montreal: McGill-Queen's University Press, 1995), pp. 13-67, 232-66.

62. "Reading of Holy Scripture," in *"Certain Sermons and Homilies (1547)" and "A Homily against Disobedience and Wilful Rebellion (1570)*," ed. Bond, p. 65.

mances of Scripture representing the divine-human paradox of the Incarnation, the "high within the low," transforming ordinary parishes into holy places for hearing the Word, for celebrating Holy Communion, and for offering public praise and obedience to God.[63]

Moreover, we may surmise that while preaching in Lincolnshire, Latimer addressed audiences whose members represented a variety of religious views, loyalties, hopes, and desires in a region that, in its majority, remained a site of contention between traditionalists and Reformers.[64] In addition to facing challenges presented by religious conflict, Latimer was ministering in a region humbled by its economic and social conditions, circumstances brought about by financial instability, unemployment, and inflation that afflicted Tudor England. Indeed, in the late 1540s, conditions in Lincolnshire were so severe that a number of parishes were combined in order to sustain a priestly ministry and essential religious activities.[65] Accordingly, Latimer's frequent references to human misery, affliction, and poverty in its spiritual and material expressions should not be seen as mere rhetorical flourishes, but rather as an expression of a vision of the Gospel addressing a severely depressed region.

Preaching the Gospel Story

In his popular preaching Latimer repeatedly turned to biblical narratives to produce sermons that were simple but lively depictions of the identity and activity of Christ and the response of Christian people united to him through faith. An example of such narrative preaching is a sermon that Latimer preached from Matthew 8:1-3, the story of Christ cleansing a leper, which he interpreted as portraying the paradigmatic enactment of salvation that produces living faith. After noting the universal appeal and application of the story, Latimer revealed his homiletic purpose by citing the words of Saint Paul: "Whatsoever is written, is written for our instruction . . . therefore if we will consider and ponder this story well, we shall find much matter in it to our great comfort and edifying" (*Works*, II. 168).

---

63. Shuger, *Sacred Rhetoric*, pp. 204-23; Wall, *Transformations of the Word*, pp. 48-49.

64. Gerald A. J. Hadgett, *History of Lincolnshire* (Lincolnshire: History of Lincolnshire Committee, 1975), pp. 168-88.

65. Hadgett, *History of Lincolnshire*, pp. 129-30. J. W. F. Hill, in *Tudor and Stuart Lincoln* (Cambridge: Cambridge University Press, 1956), refers to the isolation and ignorance of Lincolnshire as "the most brute and beastly in the realm" (p. 8).

Latimer began by observing how the preaching of Christ prompted a variety of responses, that among those who initially expressed their love to Christ were some who turned against him, dissuaded by his opponents, to whom Latimer referred as "the bishops." This particular characteristic of the Gospel story provided Latimer with a figurative way of exhorting his listeners "to never forsake God and his Word, to even suffer death for it." This move also focused attention on his primary homiletic aim, which was to position his audience to hear the story of Jesus as a call to enter and remain within the world of evangelical faith and life (*Works*, II. 169).

Latimer commended the faith of the leper as bearing witness to the significance of Christ: "So let us come to him, for he is the Saviour of mankind." He praised the leper for seeking from Christ the salvation of his body and soul, a great benefit indeed that is available to both doctors of divinity and simple folk. Latimer noted that because of his faith, the leper fell upon his knees in reverence for Christ, an outpouring of humble gratitude that challenges even the proud and the strong. Although the leper was an outcast according to the Law, he ran to Christ before any other: "Even his faith, he believed that Christ was able to help him, and therefore according to his faith, it happened to him" (*Works*, II. 168-69).

To lead his listeners to grasp the significance of Christ as mediated by the story, Latimer offered a simple explanation of how he read the Bible for preaching. He acknowledged that the Gospel reports do not simply recount historical events, but rather were written for the instruction and edification of listeners in the present. Scripture's narratives place "eternal things" before the eyes of the imagination to be grasped and enacted by faith. For this reason, the story of the leper possesses relevance for all listeners, past, present, and future, since all who hear are lepers — in body or soul — in need of the healing offered through faith in Christ. According to Latimer, this way of reading Scripture could also be applied to the story of Sodom and Gomorrah. On the one hand, it extends a call to avoid sin and wickedness, and on the other, it is an exhortation to live in a godly, upright manner. Moreover, this way of reading could be equally applied to the story of Abraham to provide an example of faith that justifies, without which God will punish the unfaithful (*Works*, II. 171-72).

In Latimer's telling of the story, the leper serves as a persuasive example of lively faith in Christ, who has promised to be with his followers always, even after his death and in his resurrection. Such lively faith continually calls upon Christ to seek God's will: "The ordinary way to get faith is through hearing the Word of God; for the Word of God is of such power, that it entereth and presseth the heart of man that heareth it earnestly" (*Works*, II. 173-74).

Latimer's announcement that living faith in Christ comes by the miracle of hearing presumably raised questions concerning the efficacy of the Word. This prompted listeners to consider if their names were written in the Book of Life, to which Latimer responded with three notes of assurance: the knowledge of sin and the feeling of one's wretchedness; faith in Christ that God will deliver through his Son; and a sturdy desire to repent and to obey God's commandments. Because the humility of faith leads to the assurance of one's place in the Book of Life, those who are willing to stand with the leper are enabled to pray, "Lord, if thou wilt." Moreover, Christ reached out to the leper — flesh to flesh — to signify his body, "eaten and drunken for salvation." According to Latimer, the ordinary means of grace prescribed by the *Book of Common Prayer* affirm that lively faith is created by the Word of God; written in Scripture, spoken in sermon, and enacted in the Lord's Supper (*Works*, II. 175-76).

Continuing to highlight the story of the leper, Latimer noted how Jesus sent the man to the temple for a priest to witness his healing, thus proving that the leper was not his own judge; his healing was no occasion for carnal liberty, proving that the preaching advocated by the Reformer was not without moral wisdom. Christ, moreover, did not disregard God's Law; his action toward the man was pastoral in nature. The lesson, according to Latimer, is that "those which find themselves grieved in conscience might go to a learned man, and thus fetch of him comfort of the word of God." Most importantly, the biblical narrative renders the capacity of Christ to evoke living faith; the joining of the leper's faith to Christ's love for him forms the basis of earnest prayer, "the art above all arts" (*Works*, II. 177).

Latimer's sermon from the story of Christ and the leper sheds light on his preaching in Lincolnshire, where his task was to induce participation in the new order of faith and obedience articulated in the *Book of Homilies* and the *Book of Common Prayer*. Conditions in Lincolnshire required that Latimer demonstrate that "lively faith" was superior to traditional religion in its truthfulness, more salutary in its practice, and more beneficial in its moral and social effects. The proof was in Latimer's performance of the biblical narrative, which rendered the presence of Christ in a manner similar to that affirmed by Erasmus in the *Paraclesis:* "These writings [Holy Scripture] bring you the living image of His holy mind and the speaking, healing, dying, rising Christ Himself, and thus they render Him so fully present that you would see less if you gazed upon Him with your very eyes."

Latimer's artful use of biblical narratives served a larger theological and pastoral aim of summoning audiences to imagine themselves within the world of the Bible, to see themselves as actors and participants in the surprising drama of salvation unfolding in their midst. Scripture, in Latimer's practice, was not simply a source to be mined to illustrate or embellish sermons; rather, all of Scripture served to disclose the character and activity of the God who commands and saves, rendering paradigmatic and persuasive patterns of Christian faith and obedience.

Although Latimer accommodated his preaching to the religious and social conditions he discovered in Lincolnshire, his discourse was primarily shaped from within the context of belief created by the official *Book of Homilies* and the *Book of Common Prayer.*[66] His robust confidence in the preaching of the word as a central means of religious and social reform was a source of encouragement to a slowly emerging evangelical minority waiting for its fruit to appear; it spurred the reconstitution of the Church Catholic in England. T. H. L. Parker writes,

> His [Latimer's] feet are planted firmly on the ground, his language is simple and direct, his thought concrete. He is concerned about such things as peace being better than war, family life better than monasteries, about servants and masters, distribution of wealth, cheating in business, and so on. But none of these is treated secularly; always it is the activity of God in the world, the relationship of God to humanity, of humanity to God.[67]

---

66. Davies, *A Religion of the Word,* pp. 231-33.

67. *The English Reformers,* ed. T. H. L. Parker (Philadelphia: Westminster Press, 1966), p. 328.

CHAPTER 5

Reformation Voices
in the Story of Sacred Rhetoric

The Protestant Reformation of the sixteenth century was, in large part, a reformation *by* preaching and a reformation *of* preaching: a reformation of the Word. Many of the Reformers were trained in the universities and religious orders of the late medieval church, where they were deeply influenced by the theological and pastoral traditions of Western Christianity. Their expressions of desire for doctrinal and practical reform were both nurtured by and protests against the wisdom of the Christian past.

Martin Luther and John Calvin are two of the most significant Reformers to be shaped by a deep yearning for the Word of God in Scripture, Jesus Christ, and whose theological and pastoral practice contributed to a strong renewal of the preaching ministry of the church. Drawing from the wisdom of the past and prompted by fresh insights derived from their contemporary struggles, Luther and Calvin are exemplars of "sacred rhetoric, the lively, life-giving power of proclamation that creates and sustains the church's identity and faithfulness to the Gospel.

Martin Luther: Theologian of the Word

For Martin Luther (d. 1546), proclamation is the center of all the church does and the central point of its theology. It is the oral address of the Gospel, both divine and human communication of God's gracious promises of salvation. In this particular form of Christian speech, the speech of

God derived from Holy Scripture and enlivened by the Holy Spirit, Christ gives himself as gift, opening the "gates of heaven" for all the continued gracious workings of the Triune God.[1]

On the altar of the city church of Wittenberg, "Luther is depicted in the pulpit, where he is pointing to the crucified Lord, exalted between the congregation and the preacher so that the focus of all will be on Christ alone, rather than the wisdom or eloquence of the human speaker. This visual expression of preaching and hearing makes clear the significance of the externality of the Word during the Reformation."[2] The preaching of the Gospel is the message of the cross, which is grasped through faith. This is the message of Christ and what he has done, which snatches listeners away from themselves, into the gracious reign of God and God's action on their behalf.

As an Augustinian monk, professor of the Bible, theologian, counselor, pastor, and preacher, Luther focused on proclaiming the Word of God heard in Holy Scripture, since God rules the world through his reliable and loving Word. It is the language of the Bible that discloses the world in a wholly particular way, the history between God and humanity witnessed by it and in turn formed by it. The divine address and human answer it evokes constitutes the goodness of life, communion itself.[3] Moreover, it can be argued that almost everything Luther wrote "preached," which may be largely attributed to the fact that his entire career was devoted to a struggle for the theological exposition of Scripture, the discipline of the sacred page that bears the imprint of God, God's will,

---

1. See the discussion in Fred W. Meuser, "Luther as Preacher of the Word of God," in *The Cambridge Companion to Martin Luther* ed. Donald K. McKim (Cambridge: Cambridge University Press, 2003), pp. 136-48; Richard Lischer, Preface, in *Faith and Freedom: An Invitation to the Writings of Martin Luther,* ed. John F. Thornton and Susan B. Varenne (New York: Vintage Books, 2002), pp. xiii-xxvii; Dennis Ngien, "Theology of Preaching in Martin Luther," *Themelios* 28, no. 2 (Spring 2003): 28-48; Brian A. Gerrish, *The Old Protestantism and the New: Essays on the Reformation Heritage* (Chicago: University of Chicago Press, 1982); Jaroslav Pelikan, *Luther the Expositor: Introduction to the Reformer's Exegetical Writings* (St. Louis: Concordia Publishing House, 1959); *Luther's Works,* American edition, ed. Jaroslav Pelikan and Helmut T. Lehmann (Philadelphia: Fortress Press and St. Louis: Concordia, 1955-86; hereafter cited parenthetically in the text as *LW*).

2. Gerhard Sauter, *Gateways to Dogmatics: Reasoning Theologically for the Life of the Church* (Grand Rapids: Eerdmans, 2003), p. 124.

3. Oswald Bayer, "Luther as an Interpreter of Holy Scripture," in *The Cambridge Companion to Martin Luther,* ed. McKim, pp. 80-82.

God's action, and God's Word, which creates the faith and life of the church.[4]

Indeed, Luther's commitment to the oral, even sacramental nature of the Word was such that he considered Holy Scripture to be an emergency measure provided by God the Speaker, a form of the "living Gospel" written in the words of the Bible as a concession to human frailty. The urgent task to which Luther devoted himself with single-minded purpose was to break open the words of Scripture so that the Gospel, the living voice of God present in Christ, the Savior and salvation mediated through the language and grammar of Scripture, "be let loose by the Spirit to reach not only the minds but the very hearts and souls of its listeners to create a faith that comes by hearing."[5]

In a sermon from John 14, Luther articulated his profound theological and pastoral vision of the Word of God — Christ himself, who works in and through the practices of the church:

> When Christ commands His apostles to proclaim His Word and carry on His work, we hear and see Him Himself, and thus also God the Father; for they publish and proclaim no other Word than that which they heard from His lips, and they point solely to Him. . . . The Word is handed down to us through the agency of true bishops, pastors, and preachers, who received it from the apostles. In this way all sermons delivered in Christendom must proceed from this one Christ. . . . For it is all from God, who condescends to enter the mouth of each Christian or preacher and says: "If you want to see Me or My work, look to Christ; if

4. See the excellent treatment of the relationship in the Reformation between Word and church in Wilhelm Pauck, *Heritage of the Reformation* (Boston: Beacon Press, 1950); Kenneth Hagen, *Luther's Approach to Scripture as Seen in His "Commentaries" on Galatians, 1519-1538* (Tubingen: J. C. B. Mohr, 1993), pp. 149-57.

5. David C. Steinmetz, "Luther and Formation in Faith," in *Educating People of Faith: Exploring the History of Jewish and Christian Communities*, ed. John Van Engen (Grand Rapids: Eerdmans, 2004), p. 259; Heiko A. Oberman, *Martin Luther: Man between God and the Devil*, trans. Eileen Walliser-Schwarzbart (New York: Doubleday, 1992); William H. Lazareth, *Christians in Society: Luther, the Bible, and Social Ethics* (Minneapolis: Fortress Press, 2001), pp. 31-57; Heiko Oberman, "Preaching and the Word in the Reformation," *Theology Today* 18, no. 1 (April 1961): 16-29; John W. O'Malley, S.J., "Luther the Preacher," in *The Martin Luther Quincentennial*, ed. Gerhard Dunnhaupt (Detroit: Wayne State University Press, 1985), pp. 3-16; Stephen H. Webb, *The Divine Voice: Christian Proclamation and the Theology of Sound* (Grand Rapids: Brazos Press, 2004), pp. 141-46.

you want to hear Me, hear this Word." . . . There you may say without hesitation: "Today I beheld God's Word and work. Yes, I saw and heard God Himself preaching and baptizing." To be sure, the tongue, the voice, the hands, etc., are those of a human being; but the Word and the ministry are really the Divine Majesty Himself. (*LW*, 22: 66-67)

Shaped by the Word

Luther's confidence in the Word of God was a gift realized through constant immersion in Holy Scripture, the fruit of a life shaped by God's judgment and mercy in Christ. The path leading to such theological understanding requires that one be interpreted by Scripture; one must therefore learn to listen and be judged by Scripture rather than standing as its judge. In the *Preface to the Wittenberg Edition of Luther's German Writings*, Luther outlines this manner of studying theology: "This is the way taught by holy king David (and doubtlessly used by all the patriarchs and prophets) in the one hundred-nineteenth Psalm. They are *Oratio, Meditatio, Tenatio*"[6] — that is, prayer, meditation, and temptation.

Prayer   The wisdom of Scripture turns all other books into such foolishness that preachers must learn to despair of their own reason and understanding, since presumptuousness leads away from eternal life and toward the abyss of hell. Rather, students of Scripture must pray with humility for the Holy Spirit, who enables, leads, and gives understanding, since prayer is a form of active waiting on the Triune God, which is mediated in the embodied word of the promise of Christ. This was the desire of David, who prayed, "Teach me, Lord, instruct me, lead me, show me," and who longed to lay hold of God, the true teacher of Scripture, in which God's economy of salvation is made known (*BTW*, 66).

Meditation   The student of theology must meditate on Scripture, abiding in the eternal Word voiced through the language and grammar of

---

6. Timothy Lull, *Martin Luther's Basic Theological Writings* (Minneapolis: Fortress Press, 1989), p. 65; hereafter cited parenthetically in the text as *BTW*. Cf. "Prayer, Meditation, Temptation," *LW*, 34: 283-88. Here I am indebted to the discussion in Reinhard Hutter, *Suffering Divine Things: Theology as Church Practice* (Grand Rapids: Eerdmans, 2000), pp. 72-75, and David C. Steinmetz, *Memory and Mission: Theological Reflections on the Christian Past* (New York: Abingdon Press, 1988), pp. 164-73.

Scripture and expressed in the practices of the church. This requires constant repetition and comparison of Scripture's oral speech and words, reading and rereading with patience so the Word and Spirit might bear fruit. This was the practice of David, who declared that by day and by night he would talk, speak, sing, hear, and read nothing but God's Word and commandments, thereby proving that scriptural meditation is not in vain (*BTW*, 66).

Temptation   Temptation is the touchstone that enables knowledge and understanding; it is an experience undergone that proves God's Word, the wisdom beyond all wisdom, to be right, true, lovely, sweet, mighty, and comforting. Those who expose themselves to God's Word, and in whom the Word takes root, are certain to provoke the devil's contradictions, assaults, and afflictions. These conditions, however, are the manner in which God makes real doctors of Holy Scripture. As Luther wrote on another occasion, "The strength of Scripture is this, that it is not changed into him who studies it, but that it transforms its lover into itself and its strengths."[7]

True theologians, who seek and love God's Word, are capable of preaching to young, imperfect Christians on the one hand, and to mature and perfect ones on the other. Such pastoral formation, the fruit of God's Word learned through the experience of faith, is necessary, since the church comprises all kinds of people in all kinds of conditions: young, old, sick, healthy, strong, energetic, lazy, simple, and wise. According to Luther, the greatest temptation for preachers is pride, or self-flattery, thinking too highly of one's preaching and seeking the praise of others, since in the book of Holy Scripture only God is honored: "God opposes the proud, but gives grace to the humble" (*BTW*, 67-68).

Luther's reading of Scripture was informed by years of monastic practice and piety, which fused serious study with prayer for the purpose of edifying faith.[8] This way of reading, which was both theological and

---

7. Cited in Bernhard Lohse, *Martin Luther's Theology: Its Historical and Systematic Development*, trans. Roy A. Harrisville (Minneapolis: Fortress Press, 1999), p. 52. See also the excellent discussion in Robert W. Jenson, "Luther's Contemporary Theological Significance," in *The Cambridge Companion to Martin Luther*, ed. McKim, pp. 282-84.

8. Oberman, *Martin Luther*, p. 172. See also Heiko A. Oberman, *The Two Reformations: The Journey from the Last Days to the New World*, ed. Donald Weinstein (New Haven and London: Yale University Press, 2003), pp. 40-43; Hagen, *Luther's Approach to Scripture*, pp. x-xi.

pastoral, was not simply for the individual but was ecclesial in scope, its goal being the unity of God and his people. Thus the importance of Luther's marks of theology — prayer, meditation, and temptation — must be understood in relation to the corresponding marks he assigned to the church.[9]

In *On the Councils and the Churches* (1539), Luther provides an account of ecclesial existence that situates preaching within the life of God's holy people, created and sanctified by the work of Christ and the Spirit. Luther begins by referring to the tablets of the law, which are written on the hearts of believers rather than stones. The first deals with the proper knowledge of God, the second with the sanctification of the body. Thus the seven marks refer to the first tablet and are to be understood as being constitutive for the church:

> That [the knowledge of God] is called a new, holy life in the soul, in accordance with the first table of Moses. It is also called the three principle virtues of Christians, namely, faith, hope and love: and the Holy Spirit, who imparts, does and effects this (gained for us by Christ) is therefore called sanctifier or life-giver. For the old Adam is dead, and in addition has to learn from the law he is unable to do it and that he is dead, he would not know this himself. (*BTW*, 543; *LW*, 41: 143-78)

Luther turns to the Apostles' Creed to define the church: "I believe in a holy Christian church, the communion of saints, that is, a multitude or gathering of people who are Christians and holy." The church is a regular assembly, a gathered people, a Christian holy people wo believe in Christ and have the Holy Spirit, who sanctifies them daily through the forgiveness of sins and also through putting off, purging, and putting to death sins, from which they are called a holy people (*BTW*, 540-41).

Christian people have the holy Word of God, the public proclamation of the Gospel of Christ, as Luther states: "We are talking about the outward word, orally preached by human beings like you and me. Christ has left this behind as an outward sign by which one is to recognize his church or his Christian holy people in the world." In addition to the externally, orally proclaimed Word of God, by which the church is recognized in the activities of preaching, hearing, believing, and confessing,

9. Hutter, *Suffering Divine Things*, pp. 75-76.

there are corresponding actions — baptism, the Lord's Supper, the power of the keys in community life (the authority of church discipline, penance, and forgiveness), the church offices and ordination, worship and instruction, and discipleship in suffering and temptation (*BTW*, 545-63). David Yeago comments,

> For Luther, these practices not only identify the church, they constitute it as church, as the holy Christian people. Luther speaks of these seven practices as *Heilthumer*, perhaps best translated as "holy things." Luther is saying, in effect, that these seven practices are true "miracle-working" holy things through which the Spirit fashions a holy people in the world. The holiness of the church is not merely a note of a purely forensic imputation to Christians of the holiness of Christ. . . . The church is sanctified by holy practices, which make up its common life through which practices the inward gifts of faith and the Holy Spirit are bestowed on the gathered people.[10]

For Luther, then, the church is constituted by God's action and not by any human action. It is a creature of the divine, external Word, into which God incorporates human witness to his Gospel by the witness of the Spirit, which makes Christian faith and life in the Triune God possible. Such holiness must be attributed to the sanctifying work of the Spirit, who authenticates human witness to the Gospel as an act of glad obedience to the First Commandment and confession of Christ as Lord, and thus, an instrument through which the whole church speaks and acts.[11] As Luther wrote elsewhere,

> I want now to come back to the Gospel, which gives us counsel and help against sin in more ways than one, for God is lavishly rich in his grace: first, through the spoken Word in which the forgiveness of sins is preached in all the world, this being the proper office of the Gospel; second, through baptism; third, through the holy sacrament of the altar; fourth, through the power of the keys; and finally through the mutual conversation and consolation of the brethren. (*BTW*, 527)

10. Yeago, "A Christian Holy People: Martin Luther on Salvation and the Church," *Modern Theology* 13, no. 1 (January 1997): 110.

11. Christoph Schwobel, "The Creature of the Word: Recovering the Ecclesiology of the Reformers," in *On Being the Church: Essays on the Christian Community*, ed. Colin E. Gunton and Daniel W. Hardy (Edinburgh: T&T Clark, 1989), pp. 118-21.

Catechetical Wisdom and Preaching

In 1528, during the official visitation of evangelical churches in Saxony, a need arose that prompted Luther to become the pastoral writer of both the Large Catechism and the Small Catechism.[12] Scholars have commented that Luther's catechisms offer the basics of his theology.[13] The material in the Large Catechism originated in 1529 as sermons on the basic texts of Christian teaching: the Ten Commandments, the Apostles' Creed, the Lord's Prayer, and sometimes the *Ave Maria*; to these Luther added instruction on baptism and the Lord's Supper. In addition, there is a remarkable coincidence between Luther's preaching and the Catechism.

The preface to the Large Catechism exhorts pastors to allow its doctrine to inform their preaching and teaching, since it "provides a brief summary and digest of the entire Holy Scripture." Although a learned doctor and an experienced preacher, Luther confessed that he continued to learn like a child, repeating each morning the Lord's Prayer, the Ten Commandments, the Creed, and the Psalms, the "ABCs" of God and his Word, to drive away the devil and evil thoughts. Since God commands such practice (Deut. 6:7-8), God himself is the Teacher. To learn the Ten Commandments in this manner is to know the scope of the Scriptures, of which the Prophetic and Apostolic writings are sermons or expositions that produce wisdom, counsel, and judgment in readers.

The Creed, moreover, is a summary of the Gospel, and the Gospel, in turn, is a narrative: it proclaims the history of God's gracious dealings with humankind in creation, the coming of Jesus Christ, and the gathering of a people, the church, through the Holy Spirit. Thus, the Creed is based on the rule of faith, and the faith of the Creed is based on the Trin-

---

12. The *Large Catechism* and the *Small Catechism* (1529), in *The Book of Concord: The Confessions of the Evangelical Lutheran Church*, ed. Robert Kolb and Timothy J. Wengert (Minneapolis: Fortress Press, 2000). See also the discussion in Martin Brecht, *Martin Luther: Shaping and Defining the Reformation, 1521-1532*, trans. James L. Schaaf (Philadelphia: Fortress Press, 1990), pp. 259-79; David C. Steinmetz, *Luther in Context* (Bloomington: Indiana University Press, 1986), pp. 85-97; Gottfried Seebass, "The Importance of Luther's Writings in the Formation of Protestant Confessions of Faith in the Sixteenth Century," in *Luther's Ecumenical Significance: An Interconfessional Consultation*, ed. Peter Manns and Harding Meyer (Philadelphia: Fortress Press, 1984), pp. 71-80.

13. Timothy J. Wengert, "Introduction," in *Harvesting Martin Luther's Reflections on Theology, Ethics, and the Church*, ed. Timothy Wengert (Grand Rapids: Eerdmans, 2004), p. 3; Steinmetz, "Luther and Formation in Faith," pp. 263-68.

ity. Because the Creed sets forth all that must be expected and received from God, it offers help in doing what the Ten Commandments require. It is summed up in three main articles that correspond to the three major divisions of the biblical narrative in its Christian Trinitarian version: "I believe in God the Father, who created me; I believe in God the Son, who has redeemed me; I believe in the Holy Spirit, who makes me holy."

George Lindbeck notes that by preaching on particular biblical narratives throughout the year, the details of this grand Trinitarian narrative are filled in. Such catechetical preaching identifies God and enables Christian people to refer to him and rightly talk to him in prayer and praise. Moreover, to learn the language of faith requires personal appropriation, *pro me*, in order to become one's own story, which elicits fear, love, and trust of God above all things, the sum and substance of the First Commandment.[14] "The Decalogue, therefore, provides the scaffolding for a form of life with the Gospel at its center, 'which teaches us to know God perfectly ... in order to help us do what the Ten Commandments require.'"[15]

Preaching the Gospel Story

Luther's preface to *A Brief Instruction on What to Look for and Expect in the Gospels* provides a concise summary of the Gospel narrative:

> Gospel is and should be nothing less than a discourse or story about Christ. ... Thus the Gospel is and should be nothing less than a chronicle, a story, a narrative about Christ, telling who he is, what he did and what he suffered. ... For at its briefest, the Gospel is a discourse about Christ, that he is the Son of God and was made man for us, that he died and was raised, that he has been established as Lord of all things. (*BTW*, 105; *LW*, 35: 117-24)

The Gospel is a book of promises. When it is opened, read, and proclaimed, Christ himself comes to listeners through Scripture and sermon, and listeners are brought to Christ: "For the preaching of the Gos-

---

14. Lindbeck, "Martin Luther and the Rabbinic Mind," in Lindbeck, *The Church in a Postliberal Age*, ed. James J. Buckley (Grand Rapids: Eerdmans, 2002), pp. 30-35. I am indebted to Lindbeck's essay in this and the next paragraph.

15. Lindbeck, "Martin Luther and the Rabbinic Mind," quoting *The Book of Concord*, ed. Kolb and Wengert, p. 411.

pel is nothing less than Christ coming to us, or we being brought to him." Christ speaks in preaching, and it is in rendering the person of Christ, the living Word, that God is his own Word. "The 'good things' in God's Word are God himself. Moreover, we become the 'good things' we hear in the Gospel by intently listening to them; with faith we are shaped to what we hear."[16] Luther concludes that the most fitting response to the gift of Christ himself is to offer one's self as an example to the neighbor, to treat him or her in the same manner Christ has dealt with the church (BTW, 108).

Sermons for Holy Week and Easter Sunday, 1529

Luther's sermons for Holy Week and Easter Sunday of 1529 offer a salutary example of his Gospel proclamation.[17] "The sermons, which were ordered according to the church's liturgical remembrance and enactment of the narrative of salvation, show Luther at his theological and pastoral best, at the height of expository power and depth of pastoral concern, preaching the Word as a 'ministry of grace and salvation.'" The sermons are also significant in that they demonstrate Luther's response to the distressing news of doctrinal ignorance, pastoral incompetence, and immoral behavior that emerged during the visitation of churches in electoral Saxony beginning in 1527. And then there was also the challenge presented by the continued presence, even in Wittenberg, of various groups vehemently opposed to his preaching and teaching.[18]

The primary emphasis of the sermons for Holy Week and Easter falls within the second article of the Creed — "And in Jesus Christ, his only Son our Lord" — which Luther interprets in the Small Catechism:

> I believe that Jesus, Christ, true God begotten of the Father from eternity, and also true man, born of the virgin Mary, is my Lord, who has redeemed me, a lost and condemned creature, delivered me and freed me from all sins, from death, and from the power of the devil, not with

---

16. Jenson, "Luther's Contemporary Theological Significance," p. 283.

17. *The 1529 Holy Week and Easter Sermons of Dr. Martin Luther,* trans. Irving L. Sandberg, annotated and introduced by Timothy J. Wengert (St. Louis: Concordia Academic Press, 1999); hereafter cited parenthetically in the text as *Sermons.*

18. Brecht, *Martin Luther,* pp. 283-92; Timothy J. Wengert, "Introduction," in *The 1529 Holy Week and Easter Sermons of Dr. Martin Luther,* pp. 13-14.

silver or gold but with his holy and precious blood and with his innocent sufferings and death, in order that I may be his, live under him in
his kingdom, and serve him in everlasting righteousness, innocence,
and blessedness, even as he is risen from the dead and reigns to all eternity. This is most certainly true. (BTW, 480)

According to Luther, "Lord" means "Redeemer." Christ has brought us
back from the devil to God, from death to life, from sin to righteousness,
and Christ alone will keep us there. The entire Gospel and all preaching
are dependent on the proper understanding of this article.[19]

Luther began his Easter morning sermon by narrating the Gospel of
the resurrection "for the sake of simple folk," so that they could hear and
believe how the story actually turned out. Inviting his listeners into the
Easter Gospel narratives according to Matthew, Mark, Luke, and John, Luther picked up the story at the point when the women arrive at the tomb
to anoint the body of Jesus, and then carried the plot forward to the startling earthquake that accompanied the resurrection. According to Luther,
"The Gospel causes an uproar in the world, but not as if this was the Gospel's fault, but rather it's the fault of the godless people. But if they can
crucify and condemn him, the heavenly Father can reawaken him during
an earthquake so that they are frightened" (*Sermons*, 119-20).

Luther's intent was to awaken his listeners with the Gospel, to summon them from death to life through faith in the risen Christ present in
the proclamation of the Easter story. Luther notes that "even the apostles were unable to see Christ alive in his resurrection, since they were
convinced that death had had the final word: to them the announcement of the angels, the external Word from heaven, sounded like an
idle tale" (*Sermons*, 121). Luther lingered at this point in his exposition to
emphasize the incredulity of the apostles, since the matter of unbelief
was also a concern for his Wittenberg listeners: "The great majority of
people listen to the resurrection of Christ like a story about the Turks.
To them it is a story painted on the wall. It must be something better"
(*Sermons*, 122-23).

Luther's homiletic aim was to demonstrate, by means of the Gospel,
that the resurrection is more than an idle tale or a painted picture that
evokes admiration and religious sentiment. Neither does Luther limit the

---

19. *The Book of Concord*, ed. Kolb and Wengert, pp. 434-35.

significance of the resurrection to what happened at a particular time and place in history; it is equally important for whoever hears the Gospel in the present. As the Lord says, "Go, and tell my brothers . . . this is what he intends with his resurrection." This intention shaped Luther's preaching. He hoped that in telling others the Easter story, the presence of the risen Christ might elicit faith's true confession: "Christ is my Savior and King" (*Sermons*, 123).

This aim also required that Luther refute the preaching of the devil, who causes blindness in those unwilling or unable to believe: "They are blind fools and look at the resurrection like a cow staring at a new gate." Although the devil's power is strong, Christ is even stronger: "He is a champion, giant and hero, who had arrayed against him the gates of hell, all devils and their cunning and death with all its powers." Thus, faith that "sees" risks everything to grasp Christ and cling to his gifts (*Sermons*, 124).

Luther's claims on behalf of the Gospel required that he deal with the reality of sin, evil, and death in light of Christ's cross and resurrection. Referring to his previous sermons on the Passion, he underscored that "Christ let himself be crucified, trampled by sin, evil and death, which were his lord" but that he concluded on a triumphant note: "But the instant when they believe him destroyed, the Lion tears himself away from sin, death, hell, and the jaws of the devil and rips them to shreds with his teeth. This is our comfort, that Christ comes forth: Death, sin, and the devil cannot hold him." Because the sin of the world has been rendered powerless, Christ's appearance to Mary is sheer life and joy. Echoing the words of Genesis 3:15, Luther proclaimed the glory and triumph of God: "Death, you shall die; Hell, you shall be defeated. Here is the victor!" (*Sermons*, 124).

Luther concluded with an exhortation to appropriate the good news of Easter, *pro nobis*: "It is a Christian art when a person can regard the Lord Jesus as one whose business is to deal with our sins." Christians are now free to look away from their sins, from evil and death, and to fix their gaze upon Christ, which is the logic or grammar of faith. "Although Christians will identify themselves with Judas, Caiaphas, and Pilate — sinful, condemned actors in the Gospel story — there is another who took the sins of humanity on himself when they were hung around his neck. . . . And today, Easter Sunday, when we see him, they are gone; there is only righteousness and life, the Risen Christ who comes to share his gifts" (*Sermons*, 125).

Preaching on Easter Sunday, Luther announced the good story, the report of the Gospel, to let loose the living Word of God, the risen Lord who rules over and in the midst of the battle between God and the devil. The focus of the sermon is the decisive action of God in Christ, the external word spoken by an angel through the apostolic witness of Scripture. Luther delivered Scripture's message with confidence in the power of the Gospel to open the eyes of even those with the most hardened hearts, the Spirit's capacity to work the miracle of hearing for which Christians now "sing, thank and praise God, and are glad forever, if only they believe firmly and remain steadfast in faith" (*BTW*, 27).

John Calvin: Homiletic Theologian

Historical Context

The preaching of John Calvin (d. 1564) was shaped by a pastoral vision of theology as a form of proclamation that aimed at interpreting God's Word to assist Christian people in living a godly life.[20] William Bouwsma has convincingly argued that "Calvin's humanist training in rhetoric equipped him to use Christian speech, shaped by the Bible, as a major instrument of reform, guided by the understanding that the language of Scripture mediates divine power to persuade human beings to right belief and transform them for right action" and that Calvin "praised what he discovered in Scripture as authored by God, because it bespoke practical, effectual knowledge of how the spiritual world operates, of how God's energy is communicated or transfused into human beings and what the embodied consequences of this transfusion should be."[21] Calvin comments on the knowledge of Christ, which is the Gospel: "For it is a doc-

---

20. Ellen T. Charry, *By the Renewing of Your Minds: The Pastoral Function of Christian Doctrine* (Oxford: Oxford University Press, 1997), p. 203. See Charry's excellent discussion of Calvin's work as a pastoral theologian, pp. 202-21.

21. Bouwsma, *John Calvin: A Sixteenth-Century Portrait* (New York: Oxford University Press, 1988), p. 113. Bouwsma's portrait presents Calvin as a historical figure who held to significant practical concerns and pastoral commitments within a larger theological framework. See the comments of I. John Hesselink, "Reactions to Bouwsma's Portrait of John Calvin," in *Calvinus Sacrae Scripturae Professor: Calvin as Confessor of Holy Scripture*, ed. Wilhelm H. Neuser (Grand Rapids: Eerdmans, 1994), pp. 209-13.

trine not of the tongue, but of life. . . . It must enter into our heart and pass into daily living, and so transform us into itself that it may not be unfruitful for us." Faith, therefore, is of the heart; it is a matter of the whole person.

For this reason, Calvin regarded the work of the Reformation as a great effort, mediated through the linguistic witness of Scripture, to transfuse the power of the Spirit, the activity of God, who speaks through the Prophets and Apostles, into human beings to hear the Word, Jesus Christ, in ways that would induce faith, love, gratitude, action, and service to God's glory.[22] T. H. L. Parker comments that for Calvin,

> The Holy Spirit is given in the preaching of the Word, giving it the spiritual power which makes it the *organum* of God's grace, so that through it is given Jesus Christ and the work which He performed for men. . . . The preaching of the Word of God is the ever renewed Revelation from God the Father given once for all in His Son Jesus Christ, mediated through the Holy Spirit.[23]

In his polemic against late medieval Scholasticism, Calvin identified himself with the attitudes and practices of Renaissance humanism, thus establishing himself as a biblical theologian committed to following and imitating the wisdom and eloquence of scriptural texts rather than coercing them with logic into an elaborately designed system of thought. Calvin described the focus of his work as "the most beautiful economy of the scriptures," the "school of the Holy Spirit," while adding that the Spirit did not adhere so exactly or continuously to a methodical plan. Divine freedom and, correlatively, the freedom of preaching that is the fruit of prayerful, disciplined learning and obedience is evinced by the paradoxes at the very heart of the Gospel, "that God became a mortal man, that life is submissive to death, that righteousness has been concealed under the

---

22. In constructing the first three paragraphs of this section, I am indebted to William J. Bouwsma, "Calvinism as Renaissance Artifact," in *John Calvin and the Church*, ed. Timothy George (Louisville: Westminster/John Knox Press, 1990), pp. 28-40; Bouwsma, *John Calvin: A Sixteenth-Century Portrait*; Oberman, *The Two Reformations*, pp. 116-29; Serene Jones, *Calvin and the Rhetoric of Piety* (Louisville: Westminster/John Knox Press, 1995), pp. 11-46; T. H. L. Parker, *Calvin's Preaching* (Louisville: Westminster/John Knox Press, 1992).

23. Cited in Philip W. Butin, *Revelation, Redemption, and Response: Calvin's Trinitarian Understanding of the Divine-Human Relationship* (New York and Oxford: Oxford University Press, 1995), p. 60; cf. pp. 102-3.

likeness of sin, that the source of blessing has been subjected to the curse" (*Commentary on John*, 18:38).

Calvin's acceptance of paradox signified not only his theological awareness of the mystery at the center of faith but also his pastoral openness to the changing realities of human experience. This humanizing effect is reflected in his work through the use of powerful imagery, imaginative insights, rhetorical elaborations, digressions, and repetitions that served a variety of biblically derived polemical, instructional, and, most importantly, persuasive purposes to promote preaching and listening as a corporate activity of the whole church. Moreover, Calvin's humanist approach as a practical theologian also made him remarkably sensitive to the concrete historical circumstances in which the Reformation unfolded. He wrote and spoke with a sense of urgency that was a major element in his rejection of speculative system-building, since he was convinced that the times called for personal and corporate response to the will of God in grateful commitment to the practical, life-shaping wisdom of salvation enacted through Scripture.[24]

Because Calvin understood his principal occupation as a first-order pastoral undertaking, the faithful exposition and teaching of Scripture to lead believers toward God, he organized the subject matter of his best-known work, the *Institutes of the Christian Religion*, into four books, each corresponding to an article of the Apostles' Creed.[25] This enabled Calvin to guide his readers — most importantly, persecuted Protestant pastors in France — to study Scripture in a manner ordered according to the Creed, the rule of faith, thus following a pastoral tradition with roots in the patristic and medieval periods, in which Christian theology was formulated from the study of the Bible according to its received doctrine for the edification of the church (*Institutes*, 1.6-10).[26] As Elsie McKee notes,

---

24. Again I am indebted here to Bouwsma, "Calvinism as Renaissance Artifact," pp. 28-30.

25. I am using the English translation of the 1559 *Institutes: Calvin: Institutes of the Christian Religion*, ed. John T. McNeil and Ford Lewis Battles, 2 vols., Library of Christian Classics, vols. 20-21 (Philadelphia: Westminster Press, 1960); hereafter cited parenthetically in the text as *Institutes*. For Calvin's purpose in writing, cf. "John Calvin to the Reader," pp. 3-6.

26. Richard C. Gamble, "Calvin as Theologian and Exegete: Is There Anything New?" in *Articles on Calvin and Calvinism*, vol. 7: *The Organizational Structure of Calvin's Theology*, ed. Richard C. Gamble (New York: Garland Publications, 1992), pp. 44-60; Charry, *By the Renewing of Your Minds*, p. 203.

"Calvin combined a theological vision of the unity, authority and practical applicability of scripture by building theology out of exegesis and guiding exegesis by theology."[27]

Calvin's theological and pastoral commitment to communion with Christ, the gift of the Spirit mediated through Scripture, sermon, and sacraments, thus dictates the scope of the *Institutes,* which weaves together the fruit of biblical exegesis into a framework of Christian meaning to promote godly knowledge and gratitude and form Christian identity and fellowship, thereby ordering the life of the church in prayer and praise to the glory of God.[28] For this reason Calvin referred to the *Institutes* as a *summa pietatis* rather than a *summa theologiae,* defining *pietas* as "that reverence joined with the love of God which the knowledge of his benefits induces."[29] Philip Butin writes of Calvin's vision of Christian worship, in which

> the initiatory "downward" movement of Christian worship begins in the Father's gracious and free revelation of the divine nature to the church through the Son, by means of the Spirit. In more concrete terms, this takes place in the proclamation of the Word, according to the scripture, by the empowerment and illumination of the Spirit. . . . The "upward" movement of human response in worship — focused around prayer and the celebration of the sacraments . . . is also fundamentally motivated by God. Human response — the "sacrifice of praise and thanksgiving" — arises from the faith that has its source in

27. McKee, "Some Reflections on Relating Calvin's Exegesis and Theology," in *Biblical Hermeneutics in Historical Perspective: Studies in Honor of Karlfried Froehlich on His Sixtieth Birthday,* ed. Mark S. Burrows and Paul Rorem (Grand Rapids: Eerdmans, 1991), pp. 224-26.

28. I. John Hesselink, "The Development and Purpose of Calvin's *Institutes,*" in *Influences upon Calvin and Discussion of the 1559 "Institutes,"* ed. Richard C. Gamble (New York: Garland Publications, 1992), pp. 209-16; Karl Barth, *The Theology of John Calvin,* trans. Geoffrey W. Bromiley (Grand Rapids: Eerdmans, 1995), pp. 158-61; John K. Mickelsen, "The Relationship between The *Commentaries* of John Calvin and His *Institutes of the Christian Religion,* and the Bearing of That Relationship on the Study of Calvin's Doctrine of Scripture," in *Articles on Calvin and Calvinism,* vol. 7, ed. Gamble, pp. 365-79; John D. Witvliet, *Worship Seeking Understanding: Windows into Christian Practice* (Grand Rapids: Baker Academic, 2003), pp. 127-49.

29. William M. Thompson, *The Struggle for Theology's Soul: Contesting Scripture in Christology* (New York: Crossroad, 1996), p. 13. See the excellent introduction to Calvin's pastoral ministry and piety in *John Calvin: Writings on Pastoral Piety,* ed. Elsie Anne McKee (Mahwah, N.J.: Paulist Press, 2001), pp. 2-34.

the indwelling Holy Spirit. In that Spirit, prayer, devotion, and obedience are offered to God the Father, who is the proper object of worship, through the Son Jesus Christ, who being fully divine and fully human is the mediator of the church's worship.[30]

The primary aim of Calvin's doctrinal and biblical interpretation was preaching, an act of worship and central activity for building up the Christian assembly (*Institutes*, 4.1-3).[31] Indeed, Calvin's most comprehensive definition of preaching's purpose is "edification," which creates and builds up the church in the knowledge and love of God, promoting an increase of holiness, thus making the Word of God useful and profitable.[32]

Yet, of all Calvin's considerable corpus of works — doctrinal, exegetical, liturgical, catechetical, and devotional — his sermons arguably are the least read and most overlooked examples of his ministry as a pastoral theologian.

In Calvin's sacramental vision of the Word, the message of Holy Scripture is the means by which Christ offers himself in his fullness to be received by faith, enlarging understanding, strengthening commitment, deepening assurance, evoking gratitude, and empowering obedience. "While the Word is the divine instrument through which Christ speaks and is spoken through the words of the preacher — God speaking — it is the Holy Spirit who effects the presence of Christ and union with him through the knowledge of faith."[33] Moreover, the activity of the Spirit embraces the human activity of edification, the pastoral and pedagogical task of fostering practices of true piety that promote sanctification and ecclesial formation, which, in Calvin's ministry, was conducted with

---

30. Quoted in Witvliet, *Worship Seeking Understanding*, p. 146.

31. Parker, *Calvin's Preaching*, pp. 1-17; John Leith, "Calvin's Doctrine of the Proclamation of the Word and Its Significance for Today," in *John Calvin and the Church: A Prism of Reform*, ed. Timothy George (Louisville: Westminster/John Knox Press, 1990), pp. 206-29.

32. Parker, *Calvin's Preaching*, pp. 17-32. For an excellent discussion of Calvin's pastoral work, see McKee, *John Calvin: Writings on Pastoral Piety*, passim.

33. Parker, *Calvin's Preaching*, p. 31; see also Leith, "Calvin's Doctrine of the Proclamation of the Word and Its Significance for Today," pp. 210-12; Eric O. Springsted, *The Act of Faith: Christian Faith and the Moral Self* (Grand Rapids: Eerdmans, 2002), pp. 182-85; Stephen H. Webb, *The Divine Voice: Christian Proclamation and the Theology of Sound* (Grand Rapids: Brazos Press, 2004), pp. 150-55. See the discussion of Calvin's developing view of faith in Barbara Pitkin, *What Pure Eyes Could See: Calvin's Doctrine of Faith in Its Exegetical Context* (New York: Oxford University Press, 1996).

building blocks quarried from Scripture. The *Institutes*, then, ordered and expanded this exegetical work to guide and inform preaching, while sermons clarified and applied the doctrine of the *Institutes* to summon the church into being, "a creature of the Word."[34]

Calvin's sermon from 1 Timothy 2:3-5 provides a perspective from which we may better understand the practice of homiletic theology as a central expression of his pastoral ministry.[35] He preached "The Salvation of All Men" in the latter part of 1554, during a time when public and political resistance was building against the reform of Geneva, and when French refugees were streaming into that Swiss city, turning to Calvin and his church for spiritual and political assistance. The conflict in Geneva involved several factions; among them were Calvin's consistory and city magistrates. The tensions came to a head in 1553, and were finally resolved in the city elections of February 1555.

There was also trouble during this time between Geneva and her more powerful neighbor and ally, Bern. Geneva wanted a treaty of alliance to be ratified: Bern was unwilling. The years of negotiations that required Calvin's involvement in Bern also caused him to interrupt his sermons on 1 Timothy, his favorite biblical book. We may conclude that Calvin's sermons from the Pastoral Epistles were delivered during a time when he, his congregation, and the whole city of Geneva were under great duress. He preached the sermons to an audience that presumably included members of the opposition, Protestant sympathizers, the undecided, and a growing number of French refugees and exiles from other European countries, thus presenting him with numerous theological and pastoral challenges.[36]

34. Leith, "Calvin's Doctrine of the Proclamation of the Word and Its Significance for Today," pp. 223-25; Edward A. Dowey Jr., "The Word of God as Scripture and Preaching," in *Later Calvinism: International Perspectives*, ed. W. Fred Graham (Kirksville, Mo.: Sixteenth-Century Journal Publishers, 1994), pp. 5-18; Ronald S. Wallace, *Calvin's Doctrine of Word and Sacrament* (Edinburgh and London: Oliver & Boyd, 1953), pp. 82-122; Healy, *Church, World, and the Christian Life*, p. 58; Christoph Schwobel, "The Creature of the Word: Recovering the Ecclesiology of the Reformers," in *On Being the Church: Essays on the Christian Community*, ed. Colin E. Gunton and Daniel W. Hardy (Edinburgh: T&T Clark, 1989), pp. 137-48.

35. John Calvin, *The Mystery of Godliness and Other Selected Sermons*, ed. John Forbes (Grand Rapids: Eerdmans, 1950), pp. 97-110.

36. Peter I. Kaufman, *Redeeming Politics* (Princeton: Princeton University Press, 1990), pp. 105-25; E. William Monter, *Calvin's Geneva* (New York: Wiley Publishers, 1975), pp. 64-92; T. H. L. Parker, *John Calvin: A Biography* (Philadelphia: Westminster Press, 1975), pp. 124-40;

Exegesis: Calvin's Commentary on 1 Timothy

In 1548 Calvin completed and dedicated his commentary on the First and Second Epistles of Paul to Timothy[37] to Edward Seymour, Duke of Somerset, who served from 1547 to 1549 as protector of England's young King Edward VI. Calvin praised Seymour for his zeal for reform and expressed hope that the duke would finish his work according to the pattern of church government laid out by the Apostle Paul to "build up Christ's Church." His comments provide a clear vision of preaching as both an activity both human and divine (CC, 181-83):

> But all these considerations ought not to hinder the ordinance of Jesus Christ from having free course in the preaching of the Gospel. Now this preaching ought not to be lifeless but lively, to teach, to exhort, to reprove, so Saint Paul says in speaking thereof to Timothy. . . . So indeed, that if an unbeliever enter, he may be so effectually arrested and convinced, as to give glory to God. . . . You are also aware how he speaks of the lively power and energy with which they should speak, who would approve themselves as good and faithful ministers of God, who must not make a parade of rhetoric, only to gain esteem for themselves; but that the Spirit of God ought to sound forth by their voice, so as to work with mighty energy . . . having liberty and free course in those to whom he has given grace for the edifying of the Church.

Calvin's verse-by-verse exposition of 1 Timothy 2:3-5 aims to convey the mind of Paul to his readers.[38] He begins by briefly discussing Paul's command to offer various types of prayers for all humanity, not only for believers: supplications, prayers, intercessions, and thanksgivings. Calvin considered such practices of prayer to be necessary for the maintenance and strengthening of the church, and for the sincere worship and fear of God (CC, 205). He summarizes Paul's message to mean that whenever the

---

Robert M. Kingdon, "The Control of Morals in Calvin's Geneva," in *Articles on Calvin and Calvinism*, vol. 7, ed. Gamble; Parker, *Calvin's Preaching*, pp. 114-24.

37. *Calvin's Commentaries: The Second Epistle of Paul the Apostle to the Corinthians and the Epistles to Timothy, Titus, and Philemon*, ed. David W. Torrance and Thomas F. Torrance (Edinburgh: T&T Clark, 1964); hereafter cited parenthetically in the text as *CC*.

38. On Calvin's method of biblical exposition, see T. H. L. Parker, *Calvin's New Testament Commentaries* (Grand Rapids: Eerdmans, 1971), pp. 49-68; David Steinmetz, *Calvin in Context* (Oxford: Oxford University Press, 1995).

church prays, its ministry should be for all humanity, even those distant and unknown, a point Paul amplifies by using three different terms that distinguish different types of prayers. Calvin views this pastoral exhortation as a sign of the Holy Spirit's work to prompt sluggish Christians, arousing and stirring them to prayer, since the call to offer thanksgiving is a form of remembering that "God makes His sun shine on the good and the bad" (CC, 205).

According to Calvin, God in his great mercy desires that Christians offer praise to him and love to their neighbors, a way of life undertaken in grateful response to the unmerited gift of divine love (CC, 206). Paul's command to pray and the rule of godly prayer also serve to remind Christians that God inexplicably but mercifully offers the hope of salvation to all without exception, and, most important, that this kindness is undeserved. God has therefore provided one Mediator for all humanity and offered access for all classes and conditions of people and nations to come to him. It is the man Jesus, the human nature of Christ, who unites humanity to God, revealing a friendly and favorable Father of all (CC, 207-8).

Doctrine: The Institutes

By examining Calvin's treatment of 1 Timothy 2:1-5 in the Institutes, it will be possible to discern the pastoral function of doctrine as the framework for biblical interpretation and its final performance in preaching.[39]

Institutes 3.20.19-20   Calvin discusses the intercession of Christ and specifically prayer in the name of Jesus. This is part of a longer section titled "Prayer, Which Is the Chief Exercise of Faith, and By Which We Receive God's Benefits," which is placed under the heading "The Way We Receive the Grace of Christ" and located within Calvin's larger discussion of sanctification. He affirms that, as faith is born from the Gospel, so too our hearts are trained through faith to call upon God's name (3.20.1). Christ is the only Mediator by whose intercession the Father is graciously rendered and easily entreated (3.20.19).

39. Richard A. Muller, "The Foundation of Calvin's Theology: Scripture as Revealing God's Word," in Articles on Calvin and Calvinism, vol. 6: Calvin and Hermeneutics, ed. Richard C. Gamble (New York: Garland Publications, 1992), pp. 398-99, 406-7.

Institutes 3.20.28   Calvin discusses two kinds of prayer: private and public. In asking of and beseeching God, Christians pour out their desires and seek those things that extend his glory and set forth his name. Christians ask for benefits, and they give thanks for the divine generosity from which every good thing comes. However, God wills that all humanity, not only the church, lift up all desires at all times, expecting and giving thanks for all things.

Institutes 2.12.1   In his discussion of "Reasons it was necessary that the Mediator should be God and should be man," Calvin again cites 1 Timothy 2:5, emphasizing that only one who is both true God and true man is able to bridge the gulf between God and humanity. Because humanity cannot ascend to God, it is God who in his majesty descends to earth. According to Calvin, the purpose of this teaching is to offer assurance that Christ, who is near, touches humanity with his life, thus sharing human flesh in its weakness.

Institutes 3.20.14   Calvin defines faith and its properties, delineating it as "recognition," a capacity to embrace what is infinite through the gift of divine revelation This revelation is truth that persuades more than instructs, truth (1 Timothy 2:4) that consists of assurance more than comprehension.

Institutes 3.20.17   Christ the Mediator and Advocate was given by God to intercede for us. Christ the Mediator comes forward as an intermediary to change the dreadful glory of the Father into the throne of grace. All of God's promises are confirmed and fulfilled in him.

Institutes 4.20.5, 4.20.17, and 4.20.23   Calvin comments that 1 Timothy 2:2 is the most notable biblical passage to speak of civil rulers. It admonishes that prayers be offered for kings and sovereigns so that Christians may lead peaceful lives with all godliness and honesty. These instructions amplify the Christian duty to offer reverent obedience to rulers, since resistance to magistrates is resistance to God, while prayers for rulers are proof of Christian sincerity.

Institutes 3.24.16   Calvin incorporates 1 Timothy 2:2-3 into his teaching on predestination in four short chapters of Book 3, "The Way We Receive

the Grace of Christ." This teaching discusses the manner in which knowledge of God the Creator and Redeemer is actualized in the life of believers
in the following order: grace, faith, regeneration, the Christian life, justifi-
cation, and last, predestination. Thus, in the 1559 *Institutes* the discussion
of predestination is placed after the exposition of grace to address the efficacy of the Gospel, an especially urgent message that would provide
hope and encourage perseverance among suffering pastors and their
churches in Calvin's native France.[40]

The function of Calvin's teaching on predestination is essentially pastoral: to address the obvious fact that all who hear the Gospel may not
believe or live faithfully, a mystery evident in all realms of life. His exposition discusses human response to grace in light of scriptural teaching, affirming that, while remaining outside human control, salvation is firmly
held in God's gracious hand. Calvin concludes that God chooses to redeem individuals for membership in the church irrespective of their mer-
its and without reference to their worthiness.[41] He cites 1 Timothy 2:3-4
to show how God deals with the reprobate (3.24.16), and he interprets
Paul's instruction to pray for kings and rulers as a reference to civil authorities who, during Paul's ministry, were intent on crushing Christ's
kingdom.

Calvin concludes that God has not closed the way of salvation to any
order of humanity, but rather has poured out his mercy so that none will
be without his grace, and that God stands ready to pardon sinners who
turn back to him. While insisting that Paul does not establish a general,
empirically evident principle of predestination, he affirms God's freedom
to include in the hope of salvation even members of the opponents and
strangers confronting the Christians in Geneva.

Calvin's concern for the welfare of the Genevan church, its ministry
with refugees, and the spiritual needs of Protestant pastors in France presumably informed his discussion of predestination in the *Institutes*. Writing for individuals and congregations who were experiencing religious
and political exile, Calvin aimed to induce trust in the divine grace that
flows from the goodness of God who knows his own, thus confirming

40. David N. Wiley, "The Church as the Elect in the Theology of Calvin," in *John Calvin
and the Church*, ed. George, pp. 113-14.

41. Alister E. McGrath, *Reformation Thought: An Introduction* (Oxford: Oxford University
Press, 1993), pp. 125-28.

the divine love that bound them through election to union with Christ: "Christ, then, is the mirror wherein we must contemplate our own election" (3.24.5). Thus the work of assurance and persuasion of election occurs through the preaching of the Word by the illumination of the Spirit to create faith in Christ and union with him: the gift of sanctification.[42] Heiko Oberman comments,

> The Calvinist doctrine of predestination is the mighty bulwark of the Christian faithful against the fear that they will be unable to hold out against the pressure of persecution. Election is the Gospel's encouragement to those who have faith, not a message of doom for those who lack it. In particular, it responds to the anguish that Calvin already felt in the early wave of persecution, which spread through Paris on the eve of his escape to Switzerland fearing that torture would force him to betray other members of his underground cell. Rather than providing grounds for arrogance, predestination offers all true Christians the hope that even under extreme duress they will persevere to the end.[43]

Preaching: "The Salvation of All Men": 1 Timothy 2:3-5

Calvin's homiletic practice was expository in nature. "The explication of Scripture makes it expository; application to the lives of Christians makes it preaching, moving from the Bible to the concrete, actual situation in Geneva."[44] John Leith argues, however, that it is not enough to speak of Calvin simply as a biblical preacher; "he was also a theological preacher who understood the divine-human relationship within the vision of a holy community called to fulfill God's purposes in history. His primary mode of articulating this vision was theological interpretation of Scripture in the homiletic performance of the Word of God."[45]

The sermon from 1 Timothy 2:3-5 begins in a rather somber tone,

---

42. François Wendel, *Calvin: Origins and Development of His Religious Thought* (New York: Harper & Row, 1963), pp. 267-77.

43. Oberman, *The Two Reformations*, pp. 114-15; cf. pp. 156-64. See also the excellent discussion of Calvin in William C. Placher, *The Domestication of Transcendence: How Modern Thinking about God Went Wrong* (Louisville: Westminster/John Knox Press, 1996), pp. 56-62.

44. Parker, *Calvin's Preaching*, pp. 97-107.

45. Leith, "Calvin's Doctrine of the Proclamation of the Word and Its Significance for Today," pp. 224-26.

which presumably reflects Calvin's perception of the conditions in Geneva.[46] His brief introduction sets forth the primary purpose of the sermon:

> When we despise those whom God would have honored, it is as much as if we should despise Him: so it is, if we take no account of the salvation of those whom God calleth to himself. For it seemeth thereby that we would stay Him from showing His mercy to poor sinners, who are on the way to ruin. The reason why St. Paul useth this argument, "that God will have all the world to be saved," is that we may as much as lieth in us, also seek the salvation of those who seem to be banished from the kingdom of God; especially while they are unbelievers. (MG, 97)

Calvin's running exposition of the text follows, expressed in a series of theological judgments and pastoral exhortations.

Significantly, Calvin's first move is to situate the Genevan Christians within the larger narrative of God's electing activity, which begins with Abraham, extends to Israel, and continues in the church for the sake of the world. Calvin announced that the Genevans had been made actors and participants in the grand story of the Triune God through the preaching of the Gospel, the grace of Jesus Christ, the Savior and Son of God the Father. He adds, however, that this new identity as children of God does not confer privileged status but rather commissions God's elect for grateful witness to the power of the Gospel, which scope embraces all nations and conditions of humanity (MG, 98-100).

For Calvin, the preaching of the Gospel is both a sign and an instrument of God's electing grace, since salvation is common to all; it is the Spirit who draws sinful people to belief, a mystery transcending comprehension. Calvin affirms what has been made known through divine revelation: God forms the speaking of his Word to fit human capacity, revelation being a divine gift dependent upon neither human merit nor worthiness. Moreover, through the activity of preaching in Geneva, the Spirit continues to call, claim, and incorporate listeners into the body of Christ, a certain sign of hope being realized in their midst (MG, 101).

Such signs of divine activity are cause for humility. It is God who shows mercy to sinners seeking forgiveness in Christ's name, sending the

---

46. Calvin, *The Mystery of Godliness and Other Selected Sermons*, ed. Forbes; hereafter cited parenthetically in the text as *MG*.

Spirit, who turns, draws, adopts, opens eyes, unstops ears, and enlightens darkened minds. Although the mystery of God's electing activity remains hidden, the Gospel does not fail to be effectual; God speaks through human words in the Spirit's voice to extend the divine will made known through the biblical narrative of Israel and Christ. According to Calvin, the fitting ecclesial response to this gracious calling is to offer God glory, to humbly give God thanks, to pray for God's continued sanctifying work, to turn from sin and doubt, and, most important, to believe the fullness of the Gospel — "that God would have all men to be saved" (MG, 103-5).

Calvin's vigorous homiletic performance of Scripture was inspired by his confidence in the Gospel: he believed that through the Spirit's power to effect the hope of salvation, effectual knowledge of God's love and favor is communicated through human speakers into human hearts (MG, 108). Accordingly, he concludes the sermon with an exhortation to pray for all humanity, repeating that God wills salvation for all nations and peoples. As an expression of this claim, he reassures the congregation in Geneva that they have been elected as God's children, that God has gathered them to himself; that Jesus Christ is the Savior of the world, the one Mediator between God and humanity; and that divine assurance will increase as they endeavor to serve others who remain afar from God (MG, 109-10).

This sermon was the pastoral fruit of Calvin's biblical and doctrinal reading of 1 Timothy 2:3-5. Focusing on the particular topic of "God wills all men to be saved," Calvin utilized Paul's teaching to persuade and assure his congregation that their election was accomplished by God's grace and loving-kindness through the preaching of the Gospel and witness of the Spirit, who calls believers into union with Christ and his sanctifying work. This news was accompanied by Calvin's exhortation for the demonstration of its practical fruit within and beyond the Genevan church: the offering of prayers on behalf of all humanity to kindle desire that the proclamation of the Word draw people from all nations and conditions of humanity into God's kingdom through Christ.[47]

---

47. On Calvin's missionary vision and activity from Geneva, see the essays in *Influence upon Calvin and Discussions of the 1559 "Institutes,"* ed. Gamble, pp. 279-334.

Back to the Future:
Re-Traditioning the Homiletic Imagination

Recalling the past and living out of it into the future has animated Jewish and Christian practice from the beginning, indeed was written into the heart of their sacred books.

JOHN VAN ENGEN

Contrary to late modern sensibilities, there are no answers in the back of this book. No new communication theory or method is proposed; no rules or principles for sermon design are provided; no "practical" tips or advice for particular strategies, programs, or steps to follow are listed. However, this just may be the most fitting way to conclude an extended conversation with exemplars of godly wisdom from the preaching tradition. They neither presumed to be technical experts, nor were they concerned with writing theory. Instead, they devoted prayerful attention to reading Scripture in light of the Christian faith to build up the church in its mission of knowing, loving, and glorifying the Triune God. This book has sketched the "grammar" or wisdom of their practice as an alternative way of discussing and evaluating preaching within the theological and spiritual tradition of the church.

My purpose, then, has been not to provide another "how to" account, but to demonstrate by enlarging the circle of our homiletic conversation that "good preaching" cannot be explained by a new method or theory. Rather, the "good sense" or "good homiletic taste" that attunes our preaching "ear" to the Word of God is acquired by participating in the ongoing struggle to know, love, and speak of God, virtues that have been displayed in the practice of wise exemplars within the Christian tradition.[1]

By engaging in serious conversation with acknowledged mentors from our Christian past, it is possible for us to live more imaginatively into the homiletic practice we share; to absorb its wisdom; to acquire a better "sense" of how it "works" as both a divine and a human activity, and as a theological and pastoral activity that locates us in God's story, drawing the world with us toward our true end: peace and friendship, communion with the Triune God.[2] Moreover, positioned within this conversation we are able to see or imagine ourselves in a new way, not simply as contemporary communicators, consumers of information, users of skill and technique; but also as members of the communion of saints, as partners in the church's company of preachers, as actors in God's story. Turning "back to the future," we may find hope in the stories, struggles, and achievements of the saints, joining them in extending the story of Christian preaching. As David Steinmetz observes, "A Church that has lost its memory of the past can only wander about aimlessly in the present and despair of the future. The Church needs the past, if only for the sake of the present and the future. . . . Only when we have regained our identity from the past can we undertake our mission in the present."[3]

Overcoming the Homelessness of Homiletics

Modern strategies that substitute convictions and forms of speech less truthful than the language and claims of the Gospel have inevitably resulted in a muteness of the church, leaving us with nothing distinctive to say, since there is no way to say it. Such loss of vital memory, language,

1. I am indebted here to Brad Kallenberg, "Retrospect: On Cultivating Moral Taste," in *Virtues and Practices in the Christian Tradition: Christian Ethics after MacIntyre*, ed. Nancey Murphy, Brad J. Kallenberg, and Mark Thiessen Nation (Harrisburg, Pa.: Trinity Press International, 1997), pp. 361-66.

2. Here I am following the thought of Alasdair MacIntyre, *Three Rival Versions of Moral Enquiry: Encyclopedia, Genealogy, and Tradition* (Notre Dame: University of Notre Dame Press, 1990), pp. 65-66.

3. Steinmetz, *Memory and Mission: Theological Reflections on the Christian Past* (Nashville: Abingdon Press, 1988), pp. 33-34. See also Robert Wilken, *Remembering the Christian Past* (Grand Rapids: Eerdmans, 1995), pp. 165-79.

and communal life has contributed to a pervasive sense of "homeless-ness" among Christian people, who struggle to maintain an alternative vision, identity, and vocation in an increasingly indifferent and even hostile world.[4] This has created a sense of living "in exile" that is not primarily a geographical phenomenon, but rather an ecclesial, liturgical, spiritual, and cultural condition. We may be geographically at home yet still "homeless."[5]

The conditions that contribute to such homelessness are reflected in the rather widespread notion that preaching is best understood as a form of "effective communication" that primarily requires one to learn and master certain techniques, strategies, and the latest "how-to" ideas that will produce immediate results. This view, however, is predicated on an explicitly technical, instrumental "grammar" of preaching that places primary emphasis on the mastery of communication strategies and techniques rather than on the acquisition of wisdom and virtue: the practice of being "mastered" or shaped by the Word of God spoken in Jesus Christ. We are encouraged to imitate contemporary "masters" in order to learn the latest "how-to" ideas, to acquire a better "delivery system" for packaging and transmitting information. But there is no mention of preaching as a Christian practice that requires lifelong immersion of one's self in the narrative of Scripture and the story of the church; no counsel for constant, prayerful attention to God in order to learn the grammar of salvation; no acknowledgment of the need to learn the language and life fitting for human beings created and redeemed to share in the grandeur and glory of the Triune God. Richard Lischer makes this observation:

> Homiletics will continue to feed this misunderstanding so long as it abstracts sermon design from the careful study of doctrine, history, liturgics, the imagination, spirituality, pastoral care, hermeneutics, and other theological disciplines, and gives to this one component the name "homiletics." . . . Without the proper grounding in *theologia*

4. Gerard Loughlin, "The Basis and Authority of Doctrine," in *The Cambridge Companion to Christian Doctrine*, ed. Colin E. Gunton (Cambridge: Cambridge University Press, 1997), pp. 51-52.

5. See the insightful essays in *Good News in Exile: Three Pastors Offer a Hopeful Vision for the Church*, ed. Martin B. Copenhaver, Anthony B. Robinson, and William H. Willimon (Grand Rapids: Eerdmans, 1999); *Exilic Preaching: Testimony for Christian Exiles in an Increasingly Hostile Culture*, ed. Erskine Clarke (Harrisburg, Pa.: Trinity Press International, 1998).

(theological wisdom), homiletics will continue as a fragmented discipline. Its exegesis will be preliminary technology rather than an exercise in prayerful dialogue with the text. Sermon design will be reduced to endless rules and formulas for high-impact communication. The sermon will be conceived as a projection of the speaker's personality or as the fabricator of religious consciousness. Preaching is thereby alienated from its home in worship, doctrine, pastoral care, and the sacramental life. *It is on its own.*[6]

Such "homeless behavior" occurs when preachers and preaching are detached from their Christian roots. This kind of activity has been described by Charles Pinches as those words or actions about which it is meaningful to ask, "What on earth could that person be saying or doing?" He convincingly argues that for an action to be intelligible, a deliberative, moral activity, it requires a home; it must fit into a whole way of life or "narrative" in which it makes sense. We are simply at a loss to make any meaningful sense of human activity that does not fit into any recognizable human narratives. Yet finding a home for words or behavior cannot amount merely to locating them in the characteristics of a particular person according to his or her preferences or decisions, a practice which has become standard for liberal cultures that privilege individual choice and consumption.[7]

Christian Preaching: At Home

This book provides an alternative vision, demonstrating by example how "Christian" and "preaching" may once again be reconciled and find themselves "at home" within a larger theological world in which doctrinal, biblical, historical, and pastoral expressions are united within a common life of knowing, loving, and worshipping God. Situated within this world, preachers draw their identity and purpose from a particular community: one that describes its speech and actions in terms of the tradition of a culture constituted by a peculiar language, wisdom, and way of life in which

6. Lischer, *A Theology of Preaching: The Dynamics of the Gospel,* rev. ed. (Eugene, Ore.: Wipf & Stock Publishers, 2001), pp. ix-x (italics added).

7. Pinches, *Theology and Action: After Theory in Christian Ethics* (Grand Rapids: Eerdmans, 2002), pp. 11-18, 158-66.

certain patterns of activity are meaningfully performed. When words and actions are extracted from their Christian home — for example, when the sermon is displaced by "culturally relevant talks" for "effective communication" — even the words of the Bible may be easily transformed into a commodity or ideology, which produce odd, homeless behaviors, distorted beyond recognition and no longer capable of accomplishing their ecclesial purposes, thus serving the powers of this world rather than God.[8]

As storied practices, Christian worship, biblical interpretation, preaching, and pastoral ministry cannot simply be redefined, revised, or reinvented to accommodate contemporary tastes. Rather, these practices call to memory and sustain Christian identity, and they are learned only when interpreted within the tradition of doctrine, devotion, and discipleship they inhabit, an ecclesial world within an ecclesial history, the shared memory of the communion of saints.[9] Accordingly, theology, or knowing and loving God, is a matter of coming to know him in prayer, worship, praise, and much else that makes up the whole Christian way of life. Theology, then, as the grammar of faith, enables us, in certain definable ways, to see, to understand, to hear, and to speak of God.[10]

Preaching so understood — as a theological and pastoral practice of the whole church — cannot simply be reduced to a matter of choice or preference, since we are not self-made creatures but a people called through the forgiving work of a gracious God. It is therefore a graced capacity for responding to and participating in the communicative activity of God: we speak because we have first been spoken by the Word, who creates and redeems all things. Such homiletic imagination, the capacity to speak truthfully, is shaped by the particular story of Scripture, its memory and hope, centered in Jesus Christ.

Through the faithful witness of the saints who continue to speak from within a living tradition, we are provided with exemplars whose lives dis-

8. On this, see Charles L. Campbell, *The Word before the Powers: An Ethic of Preaching* (Louisville: Westminster John Knox Press, 2002).

9. See the excellent discussion in Stanley M. Hauerwas, *The Peaceable Kingdom: A Primer in Christian Ethics* (Notre Dame: University of Notre Dame Press, 1983). See also Stephen E. Fowl and L. Gregory Jones, *Reading in Communion: Scripture and Ethics in Christian Life* (Grand Rapids: Eerdmans, 1991), pp. 29-55.

10. Here I am indebted to Paul L. Holmer, *The Grammar of Faith* (New York: Harper & Row, 1978), pp. 202-4.

play the necessary dispositions, habits, and judgment to hear, obey, and proclaim the Word of God. To become a preacher of the Word, therefore, is to be formed into a certain kind of character or person for service within a distinctive community; it is to be made part of the history of a practice and a bearer of its tradition; it is to acquire the intellectual and moral skills for stewardship of the Gospel and its gifts, which we have received through the work of the Spirit and the witness of our forebears.[11]

Moreover, as preachers we have been made members of a community created and sustained in holy conversation, which end is our conversion to worship, love, and serve the Triune God. "As 'storied' people, we are primarily shaped by Christian habits and skills: Baptism, Eucharist, a Trinitarian faith and way of life — the gifts and means of grace that transform us according to our vocation."[12] The cultivation of Christian character and good sense, the fruit of faith, hope, and love, enables a "knowing how" to go on speaking the truth of God, ourselves, and the world, the Living Word who is both our Way and our Home. Father Jean Daniélou affirms,

> A saint is always someone who has a sense of God's grandeur, who has found joy in God, and who, filled with his love, desires to communicate and share it, just as one would desire to speak of whatever it is that fills one's heart. If we do not speak enough about God, it is because our hearts are not sufficiently filled with him. A heart filled with God speaks of God without effort.[13]

---

11. On the theological nature of the pastoral office, see William H. Willimon, *Pastor: The Theology and Practice of Ordained Ministry* (Nashville: Abingdon Press, 2002), pp. 11-53, 331-36. See the discussion of social "characters" within a community and tradition in Alasdair MacIntyre, *After Virtue* (Notre Dame: University of Notre Dame Press, 1984), pp. 27-31. I am indebted to the excellent discussion of tradition by Stanley Grenz and John Franke, "Theological Heritage as Hermeneutic Trajectory: Towards a Nonfoundationalist Understanding of the Role of Tradition," in *Ancient and Postmodern Christianity: Paleo-Orthodoxy in the Twenty-First Century*, ed. Kenneth Tanner and Christopher Hall (Downers Grove, Ill.: InterVarsity Press, 2002).

12. Stanley Hauerwas, *Sanctify Them in the Truth: Holiness Exemplified* (Nashville: Abingdon Press, 1998), pp. 90-91.

13. Daniélou, *Prayer: The Mission of the Church*, trans. David Louis Schindler Jr. (Grand Rapids: Eerdmans, 1996), p. 97.

Index